God's Promises for Every Day

A Promise Journal

for Abundant Living

Compiled and Edited by

PAUL C. BROWNLOW

Other Books in the Brownlow Personal Reflections Collection

And Serve It With Love
Ring Bound Recipe Collectors
Country Peach Edition and Williamsburg Edition

•

Daily Planner

•

A Psalm In My Heart
Perpetual Calendar

•

Is There Life After Breakfast
Perpetual Calendar

•

Reflections for Each Day from Leaves of Gold
Perpetual Calendar

•

Family & Friends Address Books

•

For All My Special Days
Birthday Book

•

Refresh My Heart
A Daily Prayer Journal

•

Write Ideas
Blank Books

God's Promises for Every Day

Copyright © 1991
Brownlow Publishing Company, Inc.
6309 Airport Freeway / Fort Worth, Texas 76117
All Scripture references taken from the
New International Version (NIV) and used by permission.
Spiral Edition: ISBN 1-877719-30-7
Wedgewood Leather Edition: ISBN 1-877719-31-5
Plum Leather Edition: ISBN 1-877719-32-3

Contents

Precious Are the Promises

Promises are an important part of life. They are easily made, and often more easily broken. For some, a promise is nothing but a verbal ploy for procrastinating on a commitment. For a few others, a promise is still a sacred trust between parties to be kept at all costs.

I

Our Promises

In spite of the desire to keep our promises, we are not actually able to keep all of them. Sooner or later our humanity betrays us and we fail.

A. ❧ We make promises we would like to keep, but cannot physically. We promise to buy a new car, a new bike, to be back in time for the school play, etc. But we lose our job, unexpected bills come due, or our plane is late. You know all the reasons. We are sometimes physically unable to do what we planned. And we break the promise.

B. ❧ We make promises rashly and then don't want to keep them. We are fickle; we change our minds. Under the immediate emotion of the situation, we promised to do it. In the daylight of a more reasoned evaluation, we simply decide, "No, I don't want to." And we break the promise.

C. ❧ We make promises we would like to keep but later find that the price is simply too high, the commitment too expensive in time, energy, effort or even money. We struggle for a time, and then confess, "I cannot continue."
And we break the promise.

Our promises are backed up by our power or pocketbook or personality—and these finite resources can and will fail.

II

God's Promises

We break some of our promises either easily or with anguished regrets, but God is different.

A. ∾ God is not like us. God is all powerful, all knowing, all wise, all sufficient. He doesn't make empty promises or promises that require just the exact sequence of events to work out properly. He is not at the mercy of financial success, good weather or public relations campaigns.
God can and will do what He says:

God is not a man, that he should lie, nor a son of man, that he should change his mind. Does he speak and then not act? Does he promise and not fulfill?
NUMBERS 23:19

What I have said, that will I bring about; what I have planned, that will I do.
ISAIAH 46:11

B. ∾ God never quits. He doesn't keep a promise for awhile and then tire of it. His resources are never depleted. He is never exhausted by His promises even if they last an eternity:

Know therefore that the Lord your God is God; he is the faithful God, keeping his covenant of love to a thousand generations of those who love him and keep his commands.
DEUTERONOMY 7:9

C. ∾ God never changes His mind about keeping His word. He is not swayed by the whims of temporary winds. He is no fence-rider or political pragmatist. God is stable and His word is more certain than heaven and earth (Matthew 24:35):

I the Lord do not change.
MALACHI 3:6

D. ∾ God is faithful. We value faithfulness in all matters of life; marriage, employment contracts, friendships, etc. This element of God's character, His faithfulness, should speak deeply to our very souls:

If we are faithless, he will remain faithful,
for he cannot disown himself.
2 TIMOTHY 2:13

But the Lord is faithful, and he will strengthen
and protect you from the evil one.
2 THESSALONIANS 3:3

Let us hold unswervingly to the hope we profess,
for he who promised is faithful.
HEBREWS 10:23

E. ∾ God cannot lie. We honor honesty in all dealings. But even the most honest among us will inadvertently misrepresent something, or even purposefully whip up a "white lie" to avoid embarrassment. We can and do lie. God simply cannot:

God did this so that, by two unchangeable things in which it is
impossible for God to lie, we who have fled to take hold of the
hope offered to us may be greatly encouraged.
HEBREWS 6:18

III

Doubting the Promises

In spite of all the reasons and verses we have just read, most of us have had periods in our lives when we really didn't believe God was keeping His word. We were fearful, full of doubts, perplexed. Could we trust God? If so, why were we in the mess we were in? God had promised to protect us. And now look what has happened.

Doubts are not fatal or final. There is life after doubt. The problem is not our doubts, but what we do with our doubts.

Two interesting Biblical examples come to mind:

A. ∾ Gideon had given up on God. He told the stranger (the angel of the Lord), "If God was really with us, we wouldn't be in all this trouble. Where are all those great miracles we've heard about? What's happened to the God who performed all those mighty wonders our fathers told us about? God is not with us now. He has abandoned us." (Author paraphrase of Judges 6:13.)

Just then Gideon was about to be challenged with a call from God. What would he do—whine about God's supposed inactivity or arm for action?

After all the doubts we can dream up, God is still today issuing each of us a clear call to obey. He may not appear to us in bodily form, but He calls us to action. How will we respond?

B. ∾ David, the man after God's own heart, was a doubter. "Doubting Thomas" is the most famous doubter of the Bible, but one of the most frequent ones is "Doubting David."

It had been a terrible, sleepless night. David cried for help and pleaded for answers. He was so upset he could not even talk about it. Words were difficult. He thought:

Will the Lord reject forever? Will he never show his favor again? Has his unfailing love vanished forever? Has his promise failed for all time? Has God forgotten to be merciful? Has he in anger withheld his compassion?

PSALM 77:7-9

Sounds familiar doesn't it? At this point, David had two choices. He could either abandon God and go it alone, or he could remember the faithfulness of our Father and go on. Fortunately, he chose God:

I will remember the deeds of the Lord; yes, I will remember your miracles of long ago. I will meditate on all your works and consider all your mighty deeds. Your ways, O God, are holy. What god is so great as our God? You are the God who performs miracles; you display your power among the peoples. With your mighty arm you redeemed your people, the descendants of Jacob and Joseph.

PSALM 77:11-15

It's not a question of if we will ever doubt God, it's only a matter of when and what will be our response. We can continue to slip down the long slide of doubt or we can stop and remember what God has already done. The choice is ours.

IV

Understanding the Promises

One of the best ways to keep our doubts in control is to properly understand what God actually has promised. Before we can firmly stand on the promises, we must clearly understand them.

A. ❧ We must understand the proper time element.

1. Promises of the Past. Many of God's promises have already been fulfilled. His promises to Abraham, Moses and Joshua are recorded for our information and inspiration. From this history of God's faithfulness, we take confidence. But we cannot take His specific promises to the patriarchs and apply them to ourselves. We must not expect our seed to outnumber the stars or walls to fall down before us. We must be sure to determine the specific or general nature of a promise before we claim it as our own.

2. Promises for My Life. The Bible is filled with promises for God's people of all time. They are blank checks, as Charles Spurgeon has called them, to be endorsed and presented for payment. God's promises will be fulfilled—but in His own time.

Precgious Are the Promises

The Lord is not slow in keeping his promise, as some understand slowness. He is patient with you, not wanting anyone to perish, but everyone to come to repentance.

2 PETER 3:9

We think God to be slow or asleep when He is only waiting for the right time. The promise may mature only when we are mature enough to receive it. God may be too slow for our time schedule, but He is never late.

3. Promises for the Future. The end of time and the resurrection are the focus of many Divine promises. We are living by those promises and waiting for them to be fulfilled. Of such is our faith.

B. ∾ We must understand the prevailing conditions. Every promise of God has a condition except one—His promise to love us. His love is unfading and unfailing:

Let them give thanks to the Lord for his unfailing love and his wonderful deeds for men. Whoever is wise, let him heed these things and consider the great love of the Lord.

PSALM 107:31, 43

But what are my responsibilities for claiming His other promises? For example, I may feel that Satan is sucking me under into sin. I remember that God has promised that Satan will flee from me. At this moment, he is certainly not fleeing. He is devouring me. What's wrong? The full promise says:

Submit yourselves, then, to God. Resist the devil, and he will flee from you. Come near to God and he will come near to you. Wash your hands, you double-minded.

JAMES 4:7, 8

I must understand and meet the conditions for God's conditional promises to be fulfilled.

C. ∾ We must understand the appropriate method. God has promised to give us life, to sweep away our sins, to strengthen us, give us power, etc. But how? There are numerous ways He can accomplish His promises, but His ultimate method is through Christ:

For no matter how many promises God has made,
they are "Yes" in Christ. And so through him the "Amen" is
spoken by us to the glory of God.

2 CORINTHIANS 1:20

The richest, choicest blessings of God are found in Christ. To expect them elsewhere is to be disappointed and disillusioned.

V

Focusing on the Promises

This journal should help each of us focus on the
promises of God by providing:

A. A Daily Promise to nurture and encourage us. God's promises are wonderful, but we must know them and remember them to be nurtured by them. Our spiritual doubts are often caused by an inadequate spiritual diet.

B. A Journal Area to record instances of promises fulfilled or to be used as a general diary or a prayer journal, etc.

C. A Topical List of favorite promises for further study or for use in time of special need.

If we saturate our lives with the promises of God, we will worry less and live more.

....

January

*All the rivers
of Thy grace I claim,
Over every promise
write my name.*

....

I write these things to you who believe in the name of the Son of God so that you may know that you have eternal life.—1 JOHN 5:13

❧ *January 1*

God is not a man, that he should lie, nor a son of man, that he should change his mind. Does he speak and then not act? Does he promise and not fulfill?—NUMBERS 23:19

❧ *January 2*

Blessed are the peacemakers, for they will be called sons of God.
—MATTHEW 5:9

❧ *January 3*

_____

_____

_____

_____

_____

_____

_____

_____

_____

May he strengthen your hearts so that you will be blameless and holy in the presence of our God and Father when our Lord Jesus comes with all his holy ones.—1 THESSALONIANS 3:13

❧ *January 4*

_____

_____

_____

_____

_____

_____

_____

_____

_____

_____

My soul finds rest in God alone; my salvation comes from him.
—PSALM 62:1

❧ *January 5*

_____

_____

_____

_____

_____

_____

_____

_____

And when you stand praying, if you hold anything against anyone,
forgive him, so that your Father in heaven may forgive you your sins.
—MARK 11:25

❧ *January 6*

_____

_____

_____

_____

_____

_____

_____

_____

_____

For to me, to live is Christ and to die is gain.—PHILIPPIANS 1:21

❧ *January 7*

When a man's ways are pleasing to the Lord, he makes even his enemies live at peace with him.—PROVERBS 16:7

❧ *January 8*

The Word became flesh and made his dwelling among us. We have seen his glory, the glory of the One and Only, who came from the Father, full of grace and truth.—JOHN 1:14

❧ *January 9*

He will swallow up death forever. The Sovereign Lord will wipe away the tears from all faces.—ISAIAH 25:8

❧ *January 10*

For you know the grace of our Lord Jesus Christ, that though he was rich, yet for your sakes he became poor, so that you through his poverty might become rich.—2 CORINTHIANS 8:9

∾ *January 11*

_____

_____

_____

_____

_____

_____

_____

_____

_____

The Lord your God is with you, he is mighty to save. He will take great delight in you, he will quiet you with his love, he will rejoice over you with singing.—ZEPHANIAH 3:17

∾ *January 12*

_____

_____

_____

_____

_____

_____

_____

_____

_____

He himself bore our sins in his body on the tree,
so that we might die to sins and live for righteousness; by
his wounds you have been healed.—1 PETER 2:24

❧ *January 13*

_____

_____

_____

_____

_____

_____

_____

_____

Whoever humbles himself like this child is the greatest in the
kingdom of heaven.—MATTHEW 18:4

❧ *January 14*

_____

_____

_____

_____

_____

_____

_____

_____

_____

The law of the Lord is perfect, reviving the soul. The statutes of the Lord are trustworthy, making wise the simple.—PSALM 19:7

❧ *January 15*

_____

_____

_____

_____

_____

_____

_____

_____

_____

He who did not spare his own Son, but gave him up for us all—how will he not also, along with him, graciously give us all things?
—ROMANS 8:32

❧ *January 16*

_____

_____

_____

_____

_____

_____

_____

_____

_____

Without faith it is impossible to please God.—HEBREWS 11:6

∽ *January 17*

_____

_____

_____

_____

_____

_____

_____

_____

I will not forget you! See, I have engraved you on the palms of my hands.—ISAIAH 49:15,16

∽ *January 18*

_____

_____

_____

_____

_____

_____

_____

_____

_____

Consider it pure joy, my brothers, whenever you face trials of many kinds, because you know that the testing of your faith develops perseverance.—JAMES 1:2,3

❧ *January 19*

_____

_____

_____

_____

_____

_____

_____

_____

_____

_____

It is for your good that I am going away. Unless I go away, the Counselor will not come to you; but if I go, I will send him to you.—JOHN 16:7

❧ *January 20*

_____

_____

_____

_____

_____

_____

_____

_____

_____

_____

Unless the Lord builds the house, its builders labor in vain.
Unless the Lord watches over the city, the watchmen
stand guard in vain.—PSALM 127:1

❧ *January 21*

_____

_____

_____

_____

_____

_____

_____

_____

[Abraham was] fully persuaded that God had power to do what he
had promised. This is why "it was credited to him as
righteousness."—ROMANS 4:21,22

❧ *January 22*

_____

_____

_____

_____

_____

_____

_____

_____

_____

But thanks be to God! He gives us the victory through our Lord Jesus Christ.—I CORINTHIANS 15:57

❧ *January 23*

_____

_____

_____

_____

_____

_____

_____

_____

_____

For as high as the heavens are above the earth, so great is his love for those who fear him.—PSALM 103:11

❧ *January 24*

_____

_____

_____

_____

_____

_____

_____

_____

_____

Let us not become weary in doing good, for at the proper time we will reap a harvest if we do not give up.—GALATIANS 6:9

∾ *January 25*

_____

_____

_____

_____

_____

_____

_____

_____

_____

I will put my law in their minds and write it on their hearts. I will be their God and they will be my people.—JEREMIAH 31:33

∾ *January 26*

_____

_____

_____

_____

_____

_____

_____

_____

_____

For God did not give us a spirit of timidity, but a spirit of power, of love and of self-discipline.—2 TIMOTHY 1:7

∾ *January 27*

_____

_____

_____

_____

_____

_____

_____

_____

_____

The Lord redeems his servants; no one will be condemned who takes refuge in him.—PSALM 34:22

∾ *January 28*

_____

_____

_____

_____

_____

_____

_____

_____

_____

I am the resurrection and the life. He who believes in me will live, even though he dies; and whoever lives and believes in me will never die.—JOHN 11:25,26

❧ *January 29*

_____

_____

_____

_____

_____

_____

_____

_____

Have no fear of sudden disaster or of the ruin that overtakes the wicked, for the Lord will be your confidence and will keep your foot from being snared.—PROVERBS 3:25,26

❧ *January 30*

_____

_____

_____

_____

_____

_____

_____

_____

_____

If we confess our sins, he is faithful and just and will forgive us our sins and purify us from all unrighteousness.—1 JOHN 1:9

❧ *January 31*

. . . .

February

> *God has not promised us a quiet journey— only a safe arrival.*

. . . .

Who satisfies your desires with good things so that your youth is renewed like the eagle's.—PSALM 103:5

❧ *February 1*

_____

_____

_____

_____

_____

_____

_____

_____

_____

_____

He who has the Son has life; he who does not have the Son of God does not have life.—1 JOHN 5:12

❧ *February 2*

_____

_____

_____

_____

_____

_____

_____

_____

_____

_____

Remember this: Whoever sows sparingly will also reap sparingly, and whoever sows generously will also reap generously.
—2 CORINTHIANS 9:6

❧ *February 3*

Because of the Lord's great love we are not consumed, for his compassions never fail. They are new every morning; great is your faithfulness.—LAMENTATIONS 3:22,23

❧ *February 4*

I have come into the world as a light, so that no one who believes in me should stay in darkness.—JOHN 12:46

❧ *February 5*

_____

_____

_____

_____

_____

_____

_____

_____

_____

_____

A father to the fatherless, a defender of widows, is God in his holy dwelling.—PSALM 68:5

❧ *February 6*

_____

_____

_____

_____

_____

_____

_____

_____

_____

_____

Husbands, in the same way be considerate as you live with your wives, and treat them with respect…, so that nothing will hinder your prayers.—1 PETER 3:7

❧ *February 7*

The God of all comfort, who comforts us in all our troubles, so that we can comfort those in any trouble.—2 CORINTHIANS 1:3,4

❧ *February 8*

Know therefore that the Lord your God is God; he is the faithful God, keeping his covenant of love to a thousand generations of those who love him and keep his commands.—DEUTERONOMY 7:9

February 9

_____

_____

_____

_____

_____

_____

_____

_____

_____

But when he, the Spirit of truth, comes, he will guide you into all truth. He will not speak on his own; he will speak only what he hears, and he will tell you what is yet to come.—JOHN 16:13

February 10

_____

_____

_____

_____

_____

_____

_____

_____

_____

Therefore, since we have been justified through faith, we have peace with God through our Lord Jesus Christ.—ROMANS 5:1

~ *February 11*

_____

_____

_____

_____

_____

_____

_____

_____

_____

For the Lord watches over the way of the righteous, but the way of the wicked will perish.—PSALM 1:6

~ *February 12*

_____

_____

_____

_____

_____

_____

_____

_____

_____

_____

This is my gospel, for which I am suffering even to the point of being chained like a criminal. But God's word is not chained.
—2 TIMOTHY 2:8,9

❧ *February 13*

_____

_____

_____

_____

_____

_____

_____

_____

_____

_____

For God so loved the world that he gave his one and only Son, that whoever believes in him shall not perish but have everlasting life.
—JOHN 3:16

❧ *February 14*

_____

_____

_____

_____

_____

_____

_____

_____

_____

The precepts of the Lord are right, giving joy to the heart. The commands of the Lord are radiant, giving light to the eyes.
—PSALM 19:8

∾ *February 15*

_____

_____

_____

_____

_____

_____

_____

_____

_____

_____

We believe that Jesus died and rose again and so we believe that God will bring with Jesus those who sleep in him.
—1 THESSALONIANS 4:14

∾ *February 16*

_____

_____

_____

_____

_____

_____

_____

_____

_____

_____

Above all else, guard your heart, for it is the wellspring of life.
—PROVERBS 4:23

❧ *February 17*

_____

_____

_____

_____

_____

_____

_____

_____

_____

I write this to you so that you will not sin. But if anybody does sin, we have one who speaks to the Father in our defense—Jesus Christ, the Righteous One.—1 JOHN 2:1

❧ *February 18*

_____

_____

_____

_____

_____

_____

_____

_____

_____

_____

Do not judge, and you will not be judged. Do not condemn, and you will not be condemned. Forgive, and you will be forgiven.
—LUKE 6:37

∾ *February 19*

_____

_____

_____

_____

_____

_____

_____

_____

_____

I am the Lord, the God of all mankind. Is anything too hard for me?
—JEREMIAH 32:27

∾ *February 20*

_____

_____

_____

_____

_____

_____

_____

_____

_____

_____

Blessed are those who are persecuted because of righteousness, for theirs is the kingdom of heaven.—MATTHEW 5:10

❧ *February 21*

_____

_____

_____

_____

_____

_____

_____

_____

_____

_____

Having believed, you were marked in him with a seal, the promised Holy Spirit, who is a deposit guaranteeing our inheritance.
—EPHESIANS 1:13,14

❧ *February 22*

_____

_____

_____

_____

_____

_____

_____

_____

_____

_____

Commit to the Lord whatever you do, and your plans will succeed.
—PROVERBS 16:3

❦ *February 23*

Has God not chosen those who are poor in the eyes of the world to be rich in faith and to inherit the kingdom he promised those who love him?—JAMES 2:5

❦ *February 24*

Neither death nor life, neither angels nor demons, neither the present nor the future, nor any powers, neither height nor depth, nor anything else in all creation, will be able to separate us from the love of God that is in Christ Jesus our Lord.—ROMANS 8:38,39

❧ *February 25*

_____

_____

_____

_____

_____

_____

_____

_____

You will keep in perfect peace him whose mind is steadfast, because he trusts in you.—ISAIAH 26:3

❧ *February 26*

_____

_____

_____

_____

_____

_____

_____

_____

_____

_____

For where two or three come together in my name, there am I with them.—MATTHEW 18:20

❧ *February 27*

The Lord is my rock, my fortress and my deliverer; my God is my rock, in whom I take refuge.*—2 SAMUEL 22:2,3

❧ *February 28*

Because he himself suffered when he was tempted, he is able to help those who are being tempted.—HEBREWS 2:18

❧ *February 29*

....

March

> *I believe the promises of God enough to venture an eternity on them.*
>
> Isaac Watts

....

The Lord will fulfill his purpose for me; your love, O Lord, endures forever—do not abandon the works of your hands.—PSALM 138:8

❧ *March 1*

_____

_____

_____

_____

_____

_____

_____

_____

_____

Love your enemies and pray for those who persecute you, that you may be sons of your Father in heaven.—MATTHEW 5:44,45

❧ *March 2*

_____

_____

_____

_____

_____

_____

_____

_____

_____

_____

But remember the Lord your God, for it is he who gives you the ability to produce wealth, and so confirms his covenant, which he swore to your forefathers, as it is today.—DEUTERONOMY 8:18

 March 3

Now is your time of grief, but I will see you again and you will rejoice, and no one will take away your joy.—JOHN 16:22

 March 4

But because of his great love for us, God, who is rich in mercy, made us alive with Christ even when we were dead in transgressions—it is by grace you have been saved.—EPHESIANS 2:4,5

March 5

Blessed is the man who God corrects; so do not despise the discipline of the Almighty.—JOB 5:17

March 6

If you believe, you will receive whatever you ask for in prayer.
—MATTHEW 21:22

~ *March 7*

_____

_____

_____

_____

_____

_____

_____

_____

_____

The dead in Christ will rise first. After that, we who are still alive and are left will be caught up with them in the clouds to meet the Lord in the air. And so we will be with the Lord forever.
—1 THESSALONIANS 4:16,17

~ *March 8*

_____

_____

_____

_____

_____

_____

_____

_____

_____

As a father has compassion on his children, so the Lord has compassion on those who fear him.—PSALM 103:13

∞ *March 9*

I write to you, dear children, because your sins have been forgiven on account of his name.—1 JOHN 2:12

∞ *March 10*

I call to the Lord, who is worthy of praise, and I am saved from my enemies.—2 SAMUEL 22:4

❧ *March 11*

_____

_____

_____

_____

_____

_____

_____

_____

_____

If you confess with your mouth, "Jesus is Lord," and believe in your heart that God raised him from the dead, you will be saved.
—ROMANS 10:9

❧ *March 12*

_____

_____

_____

_____

_____

_____

_____

_____

_____

_____

Do everything without complaining or arguing, so that you may become blameless and pure, children of God without fault in a crooked and depraved generation, in which you shine like stars in the universe.—PHILIPPIANS 2:14,15

∽ *March 13*

_____

_____

_____

_____

_____

_____

_____

_____

_____

Praise be to the Lord, to God our Savior, who daily bears our burdens.—PSALM 68:19

∽ *March 14*

_____

_____

_____

_____

_____

_____

_____

_____

_____

_____

For the eyes of the Lord are on the righteous, and his ears are attentive to their prayer, but the face of the Lord is against those who do evil.—1 PETER 3:12

∾ *March 15*

_____

_____

_____

_____

_____

_____

_____

_____

Whoever puts his faith in the Son has eternal life, but whoever rejects the Son will not see that life, for God's wrath remains on him.—JOHN 3:36

∾ *March 16*

_____

_____

_____

_____

_____

_____

_____

_____

_____

Pride goes before destruction, a haughty spirit before a fall.
—PROVERBS 16:18

❧ *March 17*

_____

_____

_____

_____

_____

_____

_____

_____

_____

We fix our eyes not on what is seen, but on what is unseen. For what is seen is temporary, but what is unseen is eternal.
—2 CORINTHIANS 4:18

❧ *March 18*

_____

_____

_____

_____

_____

_____

_____

_____

_____

Peacemakers who sow in peace raise a harvest of righteousness.
—JAMES 3:18

∾ *March 19*

_____

_____

_____

_____

_____

_____

_____

_____

_____

Trust in the Lord and do good; dwell in the land and enjoy safe pasture.—PSALM 37:3

∾ *March 20*

_____

_____

_____

_____

_____

_____

_____

_____

_____

_____

Give, and it will be given to you. A good measure, pressed down, shaken together and running over, will be poured into your lap. For with the measure you use, it will be measured to you.—LUKE 6:38

∽ *March 21*

_____

_____

_____

_____

_____

_____

_____

_____

_____

He is like a tree planted by streams of water, which yields its fruit in season and whose leaf does not wither. Whatever he does prospers.—PSALM 1:3

∽ *March 22*

_____

_____

_____

_____

_____

_____

_____

_____

_____

*Since we are surrounded by such a great cloud of witnesses,
let us throw off everything that hinders and the sin that so easily
entangles, and let us run with perseverance the race
marked out for us.*—HEBREWS 12:1

March 23

_____

_____

_____

_____

_____

_____

_____

*Not only so, but we also rejoice in our sufferings, because we know
that suffering produces perseverance; perseverance, character; and
character, hope. And hope does not disappoint us, because God has
poured out his love into our hearts by the Holy Spirit, whom he has
given us.*—ROMANS 5:3-5

March 24

_____

_____

_____

_____

_____

_____

_____

He tends his flock like a shepherd: He gathers the lambs in his arms and carries them close to his heart; he gently leads those that have young.—ISAIAH 40:11

∾ *March 25*

_____

_____

_____

_____

_____

_____

_____

_____

_____

The word of God is living and active. Sharper than any double-edged sword, it penetrates even to dividing soul and spirit, joints and marrow; it judges the thoughts and attitudes of the heart.

∾ *March 26*   —HEBREWS 4:12

_____

_____

_____

_____

_____

_____

_____

_____

_____

A new commandment I give you: Love one another. As I have loved you, so you must love one another. All men will know that you are my disciples if you love one another.—JOHN 13:34,35

∾ *March* 27

_____

_____

_____

_____

_____

_____

_____

_____

_____

I the Lord do not change.—MALACHI 3:6

∾ *March* 28

_____

_____

_____

_____

_____

_____

_____

_____

_____

_____

Here is a trustworthy saying: If we died with him, we will also live with him; if we endure, we will also reign with him. If we disown him, he will also disown us.—2 TIMOTHY 2:11,12

∾ *March 29*

_____

_____

_____

_____

_____

_____

_____

_____

Each man should give what he has decided in his heart to give, not reluctantly or under compulsion, for God loves a cheerful giver.
—2 CORINTHIANS 9:7

∾ *March 30*

_____

_____

_____

_____

_____

_____

_____

_____

_____

The Lord is my shepherd, I shall not want.—PSALM 23:1

∾ *March 31*

April

> **If sorrow makes us shed tears, faith in the promises of God makes us dry them.**
>
> AUGUSTINE

If we are faithless, he will remain faithful, for he cannot disown himself.—2 TIMOTHY 2:13

∾ *April 1*

_____

_____

_____

_____

_____

_____

_____

_____

_____

For the Lord your God is the one who goes with you to fight for you against your enemies to give you victory.—DEUTERONOMY 20:4

April 2

_____

_____

_____

_____

_____

_____

_____

_____

_____

The greatest among you will be your servant. For whoever exalts himself will be humbled, and whoever humbles himself will be exalted.—MATTHEW 23:11,12

April 3

_____

_____

_____

_____

_____

_____

_____

_____

_____

_____

He who gives strength to the weary and increases the power of the weak.—ISAIAH 40:29

April 4

_____

_____

_____

_____

_____

_____

_____

_____

_____

_____

The world and its desires pass away, but the man who does the will of God lives forever.—1 JOHN 2:17

April 5

_____

_____

_____

_____

_____

_____

_____

_____

This is the day the Lord has made; let us rejoice and be glad in it.
—PSALM 118:24

April 6

_____

_____

_____

_____

_____

_____

_____

_____

_____

*Endure hardship as discipline; God is treating you as sons. For what
son is not disciplined by his father?*—HEBREWS 12:7

April 7

_____

_____

_____

_____

_____

_____

_____

_____

_____

*For everything that was written in the past was written to teach us,
so that through endurance and the encouragement of the Scriptures
we might have hope.*—ROMANS 15:4

April 8

_____

_____

_____

_____

_____

_____

_____

_____

_____

Bring the whole tithe into the storehouse...and see if I will not throw open the floodgates of heaven and pour out so much blessing that you will not have room enough for it.—MALACHI 3:10

April 9

_____

_____

_____

_____

_____

_____

_____

_____

If anyone would come after me, he must deny himself and take up his cross daily and follow me.—LUKE 9:23

April 10

_____

_____

_____

_____

_____

_____

_____

_____

_____

May our Lord Jesus Christ himself and God our Father, who loved us and by his grace gave us eternal encouragement and good hope, encourage and strengthen you in every good deed and word.

April 11 　　　　　—2 THESSALONIANS 2:16,17

_____

_____

_____

_____

_____

_____

_____

_____

_____

_____

For the Lord loves the just and will not forsake his faithful ones. They will be protected forever.—PSALM 37:28

April 12

_____

_____

_____

_____

_____

_____

_____

_____

_____

_____

_____

For it is by grace you have been saved, through faith—and this not from yourselves, it is the gift of God—not by works, so that no one can boast.—EPHESIANS 2:8,9

April 13

_____

_____

_____

_____

_____

_____

_____

_____

_____

My flesh and my heart may fail, but God is the strength of my heart and my portion forever.—PSALM 73:26

April 14

_____

_____

_____

_____

_____

_____

_____

_____

_____

This is the confidence we have in approaching God: that if we ask anything according to his will, he hears us.—1 JOHN 5:14

April 15

_____

_____

_____

_____

_____

_____

_____

_____

_____

_____

Praise be to the name of God for ever and ever; wisdom and power are his. He changes times and seasons; he sets up kings and deposes them. He gives wisdom to the wise and knowledge to the discerning.—DANIEL 2:20,21

April 16

_____

_____

_____

_____

_____

_____

_____

_____

_____

For we do not have a high priest who is unable to sympathize with our weaknesses, but we have one who has been tempted in every way, just as we are—yet was without sin.—HEBREWS 4:15

April 17

_____

_____

_____

_____

_____

_____

_____

_____

_____

Be careful not to do your "acts of righteousness" before men, to be seen by them. If you do, you will have no reward from your Father in heaven.—MATTHEW 6:1

April 18

_____

_____

_____

_____

_____

_____

_____

_____

_____

_____

Lazy hands make a man poor, but diligent hands bring wealth.
—PROVERBS 10:4

∾ *May 7*

_____

_____

_____

_____

_____

_____

_____

_____

_____

_____

We were therefore buried with him through baptism into death in order that, just as Christ was raised from the dead through the glory of the Father, we too may live a new life.—ROMANS 6:4

∾ *May 8*

_____

_____

_____

_____

_____

_____

_____

_____

_____

_____

If you are insulted because of the name of Christ, you are blessed, for the Spirit of glory and of God rests on you.—1 PETER 4:14

❧ *May 9*

_____

_____

_____

_____

_____

_____

_____

_____

Blessed is the man who makes the Lord his trust, who does not look to the proud, to those who turn aside to false gods.—PSALM 40:4

❧ *May 10*

_____

_____

_____

_____

_____

_____

_____

_____

_____

For Christ's sake, I delight in weaknesses, in insults, in hardships, in persecutions, in difficulties. For when I am weak, then I am strong.—2 CORINTHIANS 12:10

∞ *May 11*

_____

_____

_____

_____

_____

_____

_____

_____

_____

And I will do whatever you ask in my name, so that the Son may bring glory to the Father. You may ask me for anything in my name, and I will do it.—JOHN 14:13,14

∞ *May 12*

_____

_____

_____

_____

_____

_____

_____

_____

_____

"For my thoughts are not your thoughts, neither are your ways my ways," declares the Lord. "As the heavens are higher than the earth so are my ways higher than your ways and my thoughts than your thoughts."—ISAIAH 55:8,9

∾ *May 13*

_____

_____

_____

_____

_____

_____

_____

Submit yourselves, then, to God. Resist the devil, and he will flee from you. Come near to God and he will come near to you.—JAMES 4:7,8

∾ *May 14*

_____

_____

_____

_____

_____

_____

_____

_____

_____

A cheerful heart is good medicine, but a crushed spirit dries up the bones.—PROVERBS 17:22

~ *May 19*

_____

_____

_____

_____

_____

_____

_____

_____

_____

God is not unjust; he will not forget your work and the love you have shown him as you have helped his people and continue to help them.—HEBREWS 6:10

~ *May 20*

_____

_____

_____

_____

_____

_____

_____

_____

_____

_____

Because of the increase of wickedness, the love of most will grow cold, but he who stands firm to the end will be saved.
—MATTHEW 24:12,13

❧ *May 21*

_____

_____

_____

_____

_____

_____

_____

_____

The Lord is gracious and compassionate, slow to anger and rich in love.—PSALM 145:8

❧ *May 22*

_____

_____

_____

_____

_____

_____

_____

_____

_____

_____

The holy Scriptures...are able to make you wise for salvation through faith in Christ Jesus.—2 TIMOTHY 3:15

❧ *May 23*

_____

_____

_____

_____

_____

_____

_____

_____

_____

_____

It is written, "Man does not live on bread alone, but on every word that comes from the mouth of God."—MATTHEW 4:4

❧ *May 24*

_____

_____

_____

_____

_____

_____

_____

_____

_____

_____

Even youths grow tired and weary, and young men stumble and fall; but those who hope in the Lord will renew their strength. They will soar on wings like eagles; they will run and not grow weary, they will walk and not be faint.—ISAIAH 40:30,31

❧ *May 25*

_____

_____

_____

_____

_____

_____

_____

_____

But the Lord is faithful, and he will strengthen and protect you from the evil one.—2 THESSALONIANS 3:3

❧ *May 26*

_____

_____

_____

_____

_____

_____

_____

_____

_____

_____

For just as the Father raises the dead and gives them life, even so the Son gives life to whom he is pleased to give it.—JOHN 5:21

❧ *May* 27

_____

_____

_____

_____

_____

_____

_____

_____

_____

_____

How can a young man keep his way pure? By living according to your word. I seek you with all my heart; do not let me stray from your commands.—PSALM 119:9,10

❧ *May* 28

_____

_____

_____

_____

_____

_____

_____

_____

_____

_____

For we are God's workmanship, created in Christ Jesus
to do good works, which God prepared in advance for us to do.
—EPHESIANS 2:10

∾ *May 29*

_____

_____

_____

_____

_____

_____

_____

_____

_____

The Lord is my light and my salvation—whom shall I fear?
The Lord is the stronghold of my life—of whom shall I be afraid?
—PSALM 27:1

∾ *May 30*

_____

_____

_____

_____

_____

_____

_____

_____

_____

When you pray, go into your room, close the door and pray to your Father, who is unseen. Then your Father, who sees what is done in secret, will reward you. —MATTHEW 6:6

❧ *May 31*

....

June

*God makes a promise;
faith believes it,
hope anticipates it,
patience quietly
awaits it.*

....

The Lord is righteous in all his ways and loving toward all he has made.—PSALM 145:17

∾ *June 1*

_____

_____

_____

_____

_____

_____

_____

_____

_____

_____

Do not be anxious about anything, but in everything, by prayer and petition, with thanksgiving, present your requests to God. And the peace of God, which transcends all understanding, will guard your hearts and your minds in Christ Jesus.—PHILIPPIANS 4:6,7

∾ *June 2*

_____

_____

_____

_____

_____

_____

_____

_____

_____

Then you will call, and the Lord will answer; you will cry for help, and he will say: Here am I.—ISAIAH 58:9

∾ *June 3*

_____

_____

_____

_____

_____

_____

_____

_____

_____

Do not be amazed at this, for a time is coming when all who are in their graves will hear his voice and come out—those who have done good will rise to live, and those who have done evil will rise to be condemned.—JOHN 5:28,29

∾ *June 4*

_____

_____

_____

_____

_____

_____

_____

_____

_____

For I command you today to love the Lord your God, to walk in his ways, and to keep his commands, decrees and laws; then you will live and increase, and the Lord your God will bless you.
—DEUTERONOMY 30:16

❧ *June 5*

_____

_____

_____

_____

_____

_____

_____

_____

But now in Christ Jesus you who once were far away have been brought near through the blood of Christ.—EPHESIANS 2:13

❧ *June 6*

_____

_____

_____

_____

_____

_____

_____

_____

_____

Consider the ravens: They do not sow or reap, they have no storeroom or barn; yet God feeds them. And how much more valuable you are than birds!—LUKE 12:24

❧ *June 7*

_____

_____

_____

_____

_____

_____

_____

_____

It was good for me to be afflicted so that I might learn your decrees.—PSALM 119:71

❧ *June 8*

_____

_____

_____

_____

_____

_____

_____

_____

_____

Blessed is the one who reads the words of this prophecy, and blessed are those who hear it and take to heart what is written in it, because the time is near.—REVELATION 1:3

❧ June 9

The fear of the Lord adds length to life, but the years of the wicked are cut short.—PROVERBS 10:27

❧ June 10

For sin shall not be your master, because you are not under law, but under grace.—ROMANS 6:14

❧ *June 11*

_____

_____

_____

_____

_____

_____

_____

_____

_____

The Lord our God is merciful and forgiving, even though we have rebelled against him.—DANIEL 9:9

❧ *June 12*

_____

_____

_____

_____

_____

_____

_____

_____

_____

The name of the Lord is a strong tower; the righteous run to it and are safe.—PROVERBS 18:10

❧ *June 17*

_____

_____

_____

_____

_____

_____

_____

_____

_____

Heaven and earth will pass away, but my words will never pass away.—MATTHEW 24:35

❧ *June 18*

_____

_____

_____

_____

_____

_____

_____

_____

_____

Worship the Lord your God; it is he who will deliver you from the hand of all your enemies.—2 KINGS 17:39

∾ *June 19*

_____

_____

_____

_____

_____

_____

_____

_____

_____

Make every effort to live in peace with all men and to be holy; without holiness no one will see the Lord.—HEBREWS 12:14

∾ *June 20*

_____

_____

_____

_____

_____

_____

_____

_____

_____

_____

Therefore we do not lose heart. Though outwardly we are wasting away, yet inwardly we are being renewed day by day.
—2 CORINTHIANS 4:16

∾ *June 21*

Blessed is he who has regard for the weak; the Lord delivers him in times of trouble. The Lord will protect him and preserve his life.
—PSALM 41:1,2

∾ *June 22*

I have been crucified with Christ and I no longer live, but Christ lives in me. The life I live in the body, I live by faith in the Son of God, who loved me and gave himself for me.—GALATIANS 2:20

June 23

_____

_____

_____

_____

_____

_____

_____

_____

_____

What is man that you are mindful of him, the son of man that you care for him? You made him a little lower than the heavenly beings and crowned him with glory and honor.—PSALM 8:4,5

June 24

_____

_____

_____

_____

_____

_____

_____

_____

_____

But seek first his kingdom and his righteousness, and all these things will be given to you as well.—MATTHEW 6:33

∽ *June 25*

_____

_____

_____

_____

_____

_____

_____

_____

_____

_____

For I am the Lord, your God, who takes hold of your right hand and says to you, Do not fear; I will help you.—ISAIAH 41:13

∽ *June 26*

_____

_____

_____

_____

_____

_____

_____

_____

_____

_____

For we are God's fellow workers; you are God's field, God's building. —1 CORINTHIANS 3:9

❧ *June 27*

_____

_____

_____

_____

_____

_____

_____

_____

_____

It is impossible for God to lie. —HEBREWS 6:18

❧ *June 28*

_____

_____

_____

_____

_____

_____

_____

_____

_____

_____

For in the day of trouble he will keep me safe in his dwelling;
he will hide me in the shelter of his tabernacle and set me high
upon a rock.—PSALM 27:5

❧ *June 29*

_____

_____

_____

_____

_____

_____

_____

_____

_____

_____

All Scripture is God-breathed and is useful for teaching, rebuking,
correcting and training in righteousness, so that the man of God may
be thoroughly equipped for every good work.—2 TIMOTHY 3:16

❧ *June 30*

_____

_____

_____

_____

_____

_____

_____

_____

_____

_____

....

July

> **The promises of God are certain, but they do not all mature in ninety days.**
>
> ADONIRAM J. GORDON

....

You are no longer foreigners and aliens, but fellow citizens with God's people and members of God's household.—EPHESIANS 2:19

∞ *July 1*

_____

_____

_____

_____

_____

_____

_____

_____

_____

_____

The Lord is near to all who call on him, to all who call on him in truth.—PSALM 145:18

∞ *July 2*

_____

_____

_____

_____

_____

_____

_____

_____

_____

_____

Ask and it will be given to you; seek and you will find; knock and the door will be opened to you. For everyone who asks receives; he who seeks finds; and to him who knocks, the door will be opened.
—MATTHEW 7:7,8

~ *July 3*

Righteousness exalts a nation, but sin is a disgrace to any people.
—PROVERBS 14:34

~ *July 4*

This is good, and pleases God our Savior, who wants all men to be saved and to come to a knowledge of the truth.—1 TIMOTHY 2:3,4

∞ *July 5*

_____

_____

_____

_____

_____

_____

_____

_____

Oh, praise the greatness of our God! He is the Rock, his works are perfect, and all his ways are just. A faithful God who does no wrong, upright and just is he.—DEUTERONOMY 32:3,4

∞ *July 6*

_____

_____

_____

_____

_____

_____

_____

_____

_____

Don't you know that you yourselves are God's temple and that God's Spirit lives in you?—1 CORINTHIANS 3:16

∞ *July 7*

_____

_____

_____

_____

_____

_____

_____

_____

I am the bread of life. He who comes to me will never go hungry, and he who believes in me will never be thirsty.—JOHN 6:35

∞ *July 8*

_____

_____

_____

_____

_____

_____

_____

_____

Delight yourself in the Lord and he will give you the desires of your heart.—PSALM 37:4

∾ *July 9*

_____

_____

_____

_____

_____

_____

_____

_____

No one who is born of God will continue to sin, because God's seed remains in him; he cannot go on sinning, because he has been born of God.—1 JOHN 3:9

∾ *July 10*

_____

_____

_____

_____

_____

_____

_____

_____

I tell you the truth, whatever you did for one of the least of these brothers of mine, you did for me. —MATTHEW 25:40

∾ *July 11*

_____

_____

_____

_____

_____

_____

_____

_____

The Lord will guide you always; he will satisfy your needs in a sun-scorched land and will strengthen your frame. —ISAIAH 58:11

∾ *July 12*

_____

_____

_____

_____

_____

_____

_____

_____

_____

I can do everything through him who gives me strength.
—PHILIPPIANS 4:13

July 13

_____

_____

_____

_____

_____

_____

_____

_____

_____

Blessed are the poor in spirit, for theirs is the kingdom of heaven.
—MATTHEW 5:3

July 14

_____

_____

_____

_____

_____

_____

_____

_____

_____

Your word, O Lord, is eternal; it stands firm in the heavens. Your faithfulness continues through all generations.—PSALM 119:89,90

❧ *July 15*

_____

_____

_____

_____

_____

_____

_____

_____

Cast all your anxiety on him because he cares for you.—1 PETER 5:7

❧ *July 16*

_____

_____

_____

_____

_____

_____

_____

_____

The fruit of the righteous is a tree of life,
and he who wins souls is wise.—PROVERBS 11:30

∞ *July 17*

_____

_____

_____

_____

_____

_____

_____

_____

Salvation is found in no one else; for there is no other name under
heaven given to me by which we must be saved.—ACTS 4:12

∞ *July 18*

_____

_____

_____

_____

_____

_____

_____

_____

_____

Fear not, for I have redeemed you; I have summoned you by name; you are mine.—Isaiah 43:1

∾ *July 19*

_____

_____

_____

_____

_____

_____

_____

_____

The Lord will rescue me from every evil attack and will bring me safely to his heavenly kingdom. To him be glory for ever and ever.
—2 TIMOTHY 4:18

∾ *July 20*

_____

_____

_____

_____

_____

_____

_____

_____

_____

If you make the Most High your dwelling—even the Lord, who is my refuge—then no harm will befall you, no disaster will come near your tent.—PSALM 91:9,10

❧ *July 21*

_____

_____

_____

_____

_____

_____

_____

_____

_____

_____

Therefore, confess your sins to each other and pray for each other so that you may be healed. The prayer of a righteous man is powerful and effective.—JAMES 5:16

❧ *July 22*

_____

_____

_____

_____

_____

_____

_____

_____

_____

God is our refuge and strength, an ever-present help in trouble.
—PSALM 46:1

∾ *July 23*

There is neither Jew nor Greek, slave nor free, male nor female, for you are all one in Christ Jesus.—GALATIANS 3:28

∾ *July 24*

For the wages of sin is death, but the gift of God is eternal life through Christ Jesus our Lord.—ROMANS 6:23

❧ *July 25*

_____

_____

_____

_____

_____

_____

_____

_____

_____

_____

Wealth and honor come from you; you are the ruler of all things. In your hands are strength and power to exalt and give strength to all. Now, our God, we give you thanks, and praise your glorious name.
—1 CHRONICLES 29:12,13

❧ *July 26*

_____

_____

_____

_____

_____

_____

_____

_____

_____

_____

Therefore, since we are receiving a kingdom that cannot be shaken, let us be thankful, and so worship God acceptably with reverence and awe, for our "God is a consuming fire."—HEBREWS 12:28,29

❧ *July 27*

I will not leave you as orphans; I will come to you.—JOHN 14:18

❧ *July 28*

For his anger lasts only a moment, but his favor lasts a lifetime;
weeping may remain for a night, but rejoicing comes in the
morning.—PSALM 30:5

July 29

_____

_____

_____

_____

_____

_____

_____

_____

_____

_____

Therefore he is able to save completely those who come to God
through him, because he always lives to intercede for them.
—HEBREWS 7:25

July 30

_____

_____

_____

_____

_____

_____

_____

_____

_____

_____

The Lord...does no wrong. Morning by morning he dispenses his justice, and every new day he does not fail.—ZEPHANIAH 3:5

~ *July 31*

. . . .

August

Jesus is the yes to every promise of God.

WILLIAM BARCLAY

. . . .

The eternal God is your refuge, and underneath are the everlasting arms.—DEUTERONOMY 33:27

❧ *August 1*

_____

_____

_____

_____

_____

_____

_____

_____

_____

Therefore, there is now no condemnation for those who are in Christ Jesus.—ROMANS 8:1

❧ *August 2*

_____

_____

_____

_____

_____

_____

_____

_____

_____

For physical training is of some value, but godliness has value for all things, holding promise for both the present life and the life to come.—1 TIMOTHY 4:8

❧ *August 3*

_____

_____

_____

_____

_____

_____

_____

_____

_____

Those who know your name will trust in you, for you, Lord, have never forsaken those who seek you.—PSALM 9:10

❧ *August 4*

_____

_____

_____

_____

_____

_____

_____

_____

_____

_____

Here I am! I stand at the door and knock. If anyone hears my voice and opens the door, I will go in and eat with him, and he with me.
—REVELATION 3:20

❧ *August 5*

_____

_____

_____

_____

_____

_____

_____

_____

_____

All the prophets testify about him that everyone who believes in him receives forgiveness of sins through his name.—ACTS 10:43

❧ *August 6*

_____

_____

_____

_____

_____

_____

_____

_____

_____

There is a way that seems right to a man, but in the end it leads to death.—PROVERBS 14:12

❧ *August 7*

_____

_____

_____

_____

_____

_____

_____

_____

_____

Go and make disciples of all nations, baptizing them in the name of the Father and of the Son and of the Holy Spirit, and teaching them to obey everything I have commanded you. And surely I will be with you always, to the very end of the age.—MATTHEW 28:19,20

❧ *August 8*

_____

_____

_____

_____

_____

_____

_____

_____

Peace I leave with you; my peace I give you. I do not give to you as the world gives. Do not let your hearts be troubled and do not be afraid.—JOHN 14:27

❧ *August 9*

The Lord gives sight to the blind, the Lord lifts up those who are bowed down, the Lord loves the righteous.—PSALM 146:8

❧ *August 10*

And my God will meet all your needs according to his glorious riches in Christ Jesus.—PHILIPPIANS 4:19

❧ *August 11*

_____
_____
_____
_____
_____
_____
_____
_____
_____
_____
_____

If my people who are called by my name, will humble themselves and pray and seek my face and turn from their wicked ways, then will I hear from heaven and will forgive their sin and will heal their land.—2 CHRONICLES 7:14

❧ *August 12*

_____
_____
_____
_____
_____
_____
_____
_____
_____
_____

This is how we know what love is: Jesus Christ laid down his life for us. And we ought to lay down our lives for our brothers.—1 JOHN 3:16

∾ *August 13*

Those who cling to worthless idols forfeit the grace that could be theirs. Salvation comes from the Lord.—JONAH 2:8,9

∾ *August 14*

If you, then, though you are evil, know how to give good gifts to your children, how much more will your Father in heaven give good gifts to those who ask him!—MATTHEW 7:11

❧ *August 15*

_____

_____

_____

_____

_____

_____

_____

_____

_____

His divine power has given us everything we need for life and godliness through our knowledge of him who called us by his own glory and goodness.—2 PETER 1:3

❧ *August 16*

_____

_____

_____

_____

_____

_____

_____

_____

_____

Surely the arm of the Lord is not too short to save, nor his ear too dull to hear.—ISAIAH 59:1

∾ *August 17*

_____

_____

_____

_____

_____

_____

_____

_____

_____

Now we know that if the earthly tent we live in is destroyed, we have a building from God, an eternal house in heaven, not built by human hands.—2 CORINTHIANS 5:1

∾ *August 18*

_____

_____

_____

_____

_____

_____

_____

_____

_____

_____

In his great mercy he has given us new birth into a living hope through the resurrection of Jesus Christ from the dead, and into an inheritance that can never perish, spoil or fade— kept in heaven for you.—1 PETER 1:3,4

❧ *August 19*

You are my hiding place; you will protect me from trouble and surround me with songs of deliverance.—PSALM 32:7

❧ *August 20*

And in him you too are being built together to become a dwelling in which God lives by his Spirit.—EPHESIANS 2:22

❧ *August 21*

_____

_____

_____

_____

_____

_____

_____

_____

But when the time had fully come, God sent his Son, born of a woman, born under law, to redeem those under law, that we might receive the full rights of sons.—GALATIANS 4:4,5

❧ *August 22*

_____

_____

_____

_____

_____

_____

_____

_____

_____

When you pass through the waters, I will be with you; and when you pass through the rivers, they will not sweep over you. When you walk through the fire, you will not be burned; the flames will not set you ablaze.—ISAIAH 43:2

❧ *August 23*

Keep your lives free from the love of money and be content with what you have, because God has said, "Never will I leave you; never will I forsake you."—HEBREWS 13:5

❧ *August 24*

If the Son sets you free, you will be free indeed.—JOHN 8:36

❧ *August 25*

_____

_____

_____

_____

_____

_____

_____

_____

_____

Blessed is the man you discipline, O Lord, the man you teach from your law.—PSALM 94:12

❧ *August 26*

_____

_____

_____

_____

_____

_____

_____

_____

_____

For the grace of God that brings salvation has appeared to all men.
It teaches us to say "No" to ungodliness and worldly passions, and to
live self-controlled, upright and godly lives.—TITUS 2:11,12

❧ *August 27*

_____

_____

_____

_____

_____

_____

_____

_____

_____

Blessed are those who mourn, for they will be comforted.
—MATTHEW 5:4

❧ *August 28*

_____

_____

_____

_____

_____

_____

_____

_____

_____

For this God is our God for ever and ever; he will be our guide even to the end.—PSALM 48:14

❧ *August 29*

_____

_____

_____

_____

_____

_____

_____

_____

_____

I will forgive their wickedness, and will remember their sins no more.—HEBREWS 8:12

❧ *August 30*

_____

_____

_____

_____

_____

_____

_____

_____

_____

_____

Do not be afraid, little flock, for your Father has been pleased to give you the kingdom.—LUKE 12:32

❧ *August 31*

....

September

> *Each of us may be sure that if God sends us on stony paths He will provide us with strong shoes, and He will not send us out on any journey for which He does not equip us well.*
>
> ALEXANDER MACLAREN

....

A heart at peace gives life to the body, but envy rots the bones.
—PROVERBS 14:30

∾ *September 1*

_____

_____

_____

_____

_____

_____

_____

_____

_____

_____

He has rescued us from the dominion of darkness and brought us into the kingdom of the Son he loves, in whom we have redemption, the forgiveness of sins.—COLOSSIANS 1:13,14

∾ *September 2*

_____

_____

_____

_____

_____

_____

_____

_____

_____

_____

Not everyone who says to me, "Lord, Lord," will enter the kingdom of heaven, but only he who does the will of my Father who is in heaven.—MATTHEW 7:21

❧ September 3

_____

_____

_____

_____

_____

_____

_____

_____

_____

The Lord reigns, let the earth be glad; let the distant shores rejoice.
—PSALM 97:1

❧ September 4

_____

_____

_____

_____

_____

_____

_____

_____

_____

Therefore, if anyone is in Christ, he is a new creation; the old has gone, the new has come!—2 CORINTHIANS 5:17

❧ September 5

_____

_____

_____

_____

_____

_____

_____

_____

_____

He will wipe every tear from their eyes. There will be no more death or mourning or crying or pain, for the old order of things has passed away.—REVELATION 21:4

❧ September 6

_____

_____

_____

_____

_____

_____

_____

_____

_____

Does the Lord delight in burnt offerings and sacrifices as much as in obeying the voice of the Lord? To obey is better than sacrifice, and to heed is better than the fat of rams.—1 SAMUEL 15:22

❧ September 7

_____

_____

_____

_____

_____

_____

_____

_____

In him and through faith in him we may approach God with freedom and confidence.—EPHESIANS 3:12

❧ September 8

_____

_____

_____

_____

_____

_____

_____

_____

_____

For no matter how many promises God has made, they are "Yes" in Christ. And so through him the "Amen" is spoken by us to the glory of God.—2 CORINTHIANS 1:20

~ September 9

_____

_____

_____

_____

_____

_____

_____

_____

_____

_____

But the needy will not always be forgotten, nor the hope of the afflicted ever perish.—PSALM 9:18

~ September 10

_____

_____

_____

_____

_____

_____

_____

_____

_____

_____

So we say with confidence, "The Lord is my helper; I will not be afraid. What can man do to me?"—HEBREWS 13:6

❧ September 11

_____

_____

_____

_____

_____

_____

_____

_____

_____

So you are no longer a slave, but a son; and since you are a son, God has made you also an heir.—Galatians 4:7

❧ September 12

_____

_____

_____

_____

_____

_____

_____

_____

_____

I, even I, am he who blots out your transgressions, for my own sake, and remembers your sin no more.—ISAIAH 43:25

❧ *September 13*

_____

_____

_____

_____

_____

_____

_____

_____

_____

_____

We can have confidence before God and receive from him anything we ask, because we obey his commands and do what pleases him.
—1 JOHN 3:21,22

❧ *September 14*

_____

_____

_____

_____

_____

_____

_____

_____

_____

_____

I am the vine; you are the branches. If a man remains in me and I in him, he will bear much fruit; apart from me you can do nothing.
—JOHN 15:5

❧ *September 15*

_____

_____

_____

_____

_____

_____

_____

_____

The fear of the Lord is the beginning of knowledge, but fools despise wisdom and discipline.—PROVERBS 1:7

❧ *September 16*

_____

_____

_____

_____

_____

_____

_____

_____

_____

He has given us his very great and precious promises, so that through them you may participate in the divine nature and escape the corruption in the world caused by evil desires.—2 PETER 1:4

☙ *September 17*

...remembering the words of the Lord Jesus: "It is more blessed to give than to receive."—ACTS 20:35

☙ *September 18*

The sun will no more be your light by day, nor will the brightness of the moon shine on you, for the Lord will be your everlasting light, and your God will be your glory.—ISAIAH 60:19

∾ *September 19*

_____

_____

_____

_____

_____

_____

_____

_____

_____

_____

God is faithful; he will not let you be tempted beyond what you can bear. But when you are tempted, he will also provide a way out so that you can stand up under it.—1 CORINTHIANS 10:13

∾ *September 20*

_____

_____

_____

_____

_____

_____

_____

_____

_____

_____

"If you can?" said Jesus. Everything is possible for him who believes.—MARK 9:23

❧ *September 21*

_____

_____

_____

_____

_____

_____

_____

_____

_____

_____

Who is a God like you, who pardons sin and forgives the transgression of the remnant of his inheritance? You do not stay angry forever but delight to show mercy.—MICAH 7:18

❧ *September 22*

_____

_____

_____

_____

_____

_____

_____

_____

_____

And if the Spirit of him who raised Jesus from the dead is living in you, he who raised Christ from the dead will also give life to your mortal bodies through his Spirit, who lives in you.—ROMANS 8:11

❧ *September 23*

For the love of money is a root of all kinds of evil. Some people, eager for money, have wandered from the faith and pierced themselves with many griefs.—1 TIMOTHY 6:10

❧ *September 24*

If your enemy is hungry, give him food to eat; if he is thirsty, give him water to drink. In doing this, you will heap burning coals on his head, and the Lord will reward you.—PROVERBS 25:21,22

❧ September 25

_____

_____

_____

_____

_____

_____

_____

_____

_____

For you have been born again, not of perishable seed, but imperishable, through the living and enduring word of God.
—1 PETER 1:23

❧ September 26

_____

_____

_____

_____

_____

_____

_____

_____

_____

Blessed are the meek, for they will inherit the earth.—MATTHEW 5:5

❧ *September 27*

_____

_____

_____

_____

_____

_____

_____

_____

_____

Many are the woes of the wicked, but the Lord's unfailing love surrounds the man who trusts in him.—PSALM 32:10

❧ *September 28*

_____

_____

_____

_____

_____

_____

_____

_____

_____

Christ is the mediator of a new covenant, that those who are called may receive the promised eternal inheritance.—HEBREWS 9:15

❧ *September 29*

Sell your possessions and give to the poor. Provide purses for yourselves that will not wear out, a treasure in heaven that will not be exhausted, where no thief comes near and no moth destroys. For where your treasure is, there your heart will be also.—LUKE 12:33,34

❧ *September 30*

....

October

> **The Lord promised His disciples three things: they would be entirely fearless, absurdly happy, and always in trouble.**
>
> T.R. GLOVER

....

Cast your cares on the Lord and he will sustain you; he will never let the righteous fall.—PSALM 55:22

⸎ *October 1*

_____

_____

_____

_____

_____

_____

_____

_____

_____

_____

He has reconciled you by Christ's physical body through death to present you holy in his sight, without blemish and free from accusation.—COLOSSIANS 1:22

⸎ *October 2*

_____

_____

_____

_____

_____

_____

_____

_____

_____

You will again have compassion on us; you will tread our sins underfoot and hurl all our iniquities into the depths of the sea.
—MICAH 7:19

∾ *October 3*

_____

_____

_____

_____

_____

_____

_____

_____

The thief comes only to steal and kill and destroy; I have come that they may have life, and have it to the full.—JOHN 10:10

∾ *October 4*

_____

_____

_____

_____

_____

_____

_____

_____

The Lord your God is gracious and compassionate. He will not turn his face from you if you return to him.—2 CHRONICLES 30:9

❧ *October 5*

_____

_____

_____

_____

_____

_____

_____

_____

_____

_____

...but to put their hope in God, who richly provides us with everything for our enjoyment.—1 TIMOTHY 6:17

❧ *October 6*

_____

_____

_____

_____

_____

_____

_____

_____

_____

_____

_____

God made him who had no sin to be sin for us, so that in him we might become the righteousness of God.—2 CORINTHIANS 5:21

❧ *October 7*

_____

_____

_____

_____

_____

_____

_____

_____

_____

_____

The angel of the Lord encamps around those who fear him, and he delivers them.—PSALM 34:7

❧ *October 8*

_____

_____

_____

_____

_____

_____

_____

_____

_____

_____

Dear children,…the one who is in you is greater than the one who is in the world.—1 JOHN 4:4

❧ *October 9*

_____

_____

_____

_____

_____

_____

_____

_____

_____

Christ was sacrificed once to take away the sins of many people; and he will appear a second time, not to bear sin, but to bring salvation to those who are waiting for him.—HEBREWS 9:28

❧ *October 10*

_____

_____

_____

_____

_____

_____

_____

_____

_____

_____

*Be strong and courageous. Do not be terrified; do not be discouraged,
for the Lord your God will be with you wherever you go.*
—JOSHUA 1:9

❧ *October 11*

_____

_____

_____

_____

_____

_____

_____

_____

_____

*If you remain in me and my words remain in you, ask whatever you
wish, and it will be given you.*—JOHN 15:7

❧ *October 12*

_____

_____

_____

_____

_____

_____

_____

_____

_____

_____

Sitting down, Jesus called the Twelve and said, "If anyone wants to be first, he must be the very last, and the servant of all."

—MARK 9:35

❧ *October 13*

_____

_____

_____

_____

_____

_____

_____

_____

_____

I will pour out my Spirit on all people. Your sons and daughters will prophesy, your old men will dream dreams, your young men will see visions.—JOEL 2:28

❧ *October 14*

_____

_____

_____

_____

_____

_____

_____

_____

_____

The Lord is not slow in keeping his promise, as some understand slowness. He is patient with you, not wanting anyone to perish, but everyone to come to repentance.—2 PETER 3:9

❧ *October 15*

Blessed are those who hunger and thirst for righteousness, for they will be filled.—MATTHEW 5:6

❧ *October 16*

Know that the Lord is God. It is he who made us, and we are his.
—PSALM 100:3

❧ *October 17*

_____

_____

_____

_____

_____

_____

_____

_____

_____

Now to him who is able to do immeasurably more than all we ask or imagine, according to his power that is at work within us, to him be glory in the church and in Christ Jesus throughout all generations, for ever and ever!—EPHESIANS 3:20,21

❧ *October 18*

_____

_____

_____

_____

_____

_____

_____

_____

Come to me, all you who are weary and burdened, and I will give you rest.—MATTHEW 11:28

∾ *October 19*

_____

_____

_____

_____

_____

_____

_____

_____

_____

Behold, I will create new heavens and a new earth. The former things will not be remembered, nor will they come to mind.
—ISAIAH 65:17

∾ *October 20*

_____

_____

_____

_____

_____

_____

_____

_____

_____

Jesus Christ is the same yesterday and today and forever.
—HEBREWS 13:8

❧ *October 21*

_____

_____

_____

_____

_____

_____

_____

_____

_____

_____

Do not boast about tomorrow, for you do not know what a day may bring forth.—PROVERBS 27:1

❧ *October 22*

_____

_____

_____

_____

_____

_____

_____

_____

_____

_____

For you did not receive a spirit that makes you a slave again to fear, but you received the Spirit who makes you sons. And by him we cry, "Abba, Father."—ROMANS 8:15

❧ *October 23*

_____

_____

_____

_____

_____

_____

_____

_____

_____

Trust in the Lord with all your heart and lean not on your own understanding; in all your ways acknowledge him, and he will make your paths straight.—PROVERBS 3:5,6

❧ *October 24*

_____

_____

_____

_____

_____

_____

_____

_____

_____

But the fruit of the Spirit is love, joy, peace, patience, kindness, goodness, faithfulness, gentleness and self-control.
—GALATIANS 5:22,23

❧ *October 25*

_____

_____

_____

_____

_____

_____

_____

_____

_____

_____

I am not ashamed of the gospel, because it is the power of God for the salvation of everyone who believes: first for the Jew, then for the Gentile.—ROMANS 1:16

❧ *October 26*

_____

_____

_____

_____

_____

_____

_____

_____

_____

_____

I lift up my eyes to the hills—where does my help come from? My help comes from the Lord, the Maker of heaven and earth.
—PSALM 121:1,2

∾ *October 27*

_____

_____

_____

_____

_____

_____

_____

_____

_____

By one sacrifice he has made perfect forever those who are being made holy—HEBREWS 10:14

∾ *October 28*

_____

_____

_____

_____

_____

_____

_____

_____

_____

But when you give a banquet, invite the poor, the crippled, the lame, the blind, and you will be blessed. Although they cannot repay you, you will be repaid at the resurrection of the righteous.
—LUKE 14:13,14

❧ *October 29*

_____

_____

_____

_____

_____

_____

_____

_____

_____

I have swept away your offenses like a cloud, your sins like the morning mist. Return to me, for I have redeemed you.—ISAIAH 44:22

❧ *October 30*

_____

_____

_____

_____

_____

_____

_____

_____

_____

There are different kinds of spiritual gifts, but the same Spirit. There are different kinds of service, but the same Lord. There are different kinds of working, but the same God works all of them in all men.—1 CORINTHIANS 12:4-6

❧ October 31

November

> *God has given no pledge which He will not redeem, and encouraged no hope which He will not fulfill.*
>
> CHARLES H. SPURGEON

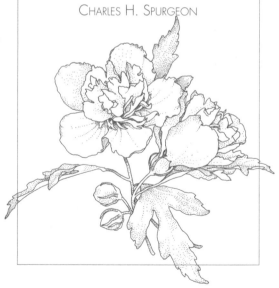

....

The Lord is good, a refuge in times of trouble. He cares for those who trust in him.—NAHUM 1:7

∾ *November 1*

_____

_____

_____

_____

_____

_____

_____

_____

_____

For in Christ all the fullness of the Deity lives in bodily form, and you have this fullness in Christ, who is the head over every power and authority.—COLOSSIANS 2:9,10

∾ *November 2*

_____

_____

_____

_____

_____

_____

_____

_____

_____

What I have said, that will I bring about; what I have planned, that will I do.—ISAIAH 46:11

❧ *November 3*

_____

_____

_____

_____

_____

_____

_____

_____

_____

_____

I tell you the truth, anyone who will not receive the kingdom of God like a little child will never enter it.—MARK 10:15

❧ *November 4*

_____

_____

_____

_____

_____

_____

_____

_____

_____

_____

*The Lord will keep you from all harm—he will watch over your life;
the Lord will watch over your coming and going both now and
forevermore.*—PSALM 121:7,8

November 5

_____

_____

_____

_____

_____

_____

_____

_____

_____

_____

*But you are a chosen people, a royal priesthood, a holy nation, a
people belonging to God, that you may declare the praises of him who
called you out of darkness into his wonderful light.*—1 PETER 2:9

November 6

_____

_____

_____

_____

_____

_____

_____

_____

_____

_____

_____

Blessed are the merciful, for they will be shown mercy.
—MATTHEW 5:7

ॐ November 7

As a mother comforts her child, so will I comfort you.—ISAIAH 66:13

ॐ November 8

And do not forget to do good and to share with others, for with such sacrifices God is pleased.—HEBREWS 13:16

❧ *November 9*

_____

_____

_____

_____

_____

_____

_____

_____

_____

But the day of the Lord will come like a thief. The heavens will disappear with a roar; the elements will be destroyed by fire, and the earth and everything in it will be laid bare.—2 PETER 3:10

❧ *November 10*

_____

_____

_____

_____

_____

_____

_____

_____

_____

For the Lord is good and his love endures forever; his faithfulness
continues through all generations.—PSALM 100:5

❧ *November 11*

_____

_____

_____

_____

_____

_____

_____

_____

_____

_____

For whoever does the will of my Father in heaven is my brother and
sister and mother.—MATTHEW 12:50

❧ *November 12*

_____

_____

_____

_____

_____

_____

_____

_____

_____

There is no one holy like the Lord; there is no one besides you; there is no Rock like our God.—1 SAMUEL 2:2

❧ *November 13*

_____

_____

_____

_____

_____

_____

_____

_____

Dear friends, let us love one another, for love comes from God. Everyone who loves has been born of God and knows God.
—1 JOHN 4:7

❧ *November 14*

_____

_____

_____

_____

_____

_____

_____

_____

_____

With him is only the arm of flesh, but with us is the Lord our God to help us and to fight our battles. —2 CHRONICLES 32:8

❧ *November 15*

_____

_____

_____

_____

_____

_____

_____

_____

The Son is the radiance of God's glory and the exact representation of his being, sustaining all things by his powerful word.
—HEBREWS 1:3

❧ *November 16*

_____

_____

_____

_____

_____

_____

_____

_____

Do not be deceived: God cannot be mocked. A man reaps what he sows.—GALATIANS 6:7

✿ *November 17*

_____

_____

_____

_____

_____

_____

_____

_____

Better a meal of vegetables where there is love than a fatted calf with hatred.—PROVERBS 15:17

✿ *November 18*

_____

_____

_____

_____

_____

_____

_____

_____

_____

Command them to do good, to be rich in good deeds, and to be generous and willing to share. In this way they will lay up treasure for themselves.—1 TIMOTHY 6:18,19

❧ *November 19*

_____

_____

_____

_____

_____

_____

_____

_____

_____

_____

And now these three remain: faith, hope and love. But the greatest of these is love.—1 CORINTHIANS 13:13

❧ *November 20*

_____

_____

_____

_____

_____

_____

_____

_____

_____

_____

The eyes of the Lord are on the righteous and his ears are attentive to their cry.—PSALM 34:15

∾ *November 21*

Therefore come out from them and be separate, says the Lord. Touch no unclean thing, and I will receive you. I will be a Father to you, and you will be my sons and daughters, says the Lord Almighty.
—2 CORINTHIANS 6:17,18

∾ *November 22*

For in the gospel a righteousness from God is revealed, a righteousness that is by faith from first to last, just as it is written: "The righteous will live by faith."—ROMANS 1:17

❧ *November 23*

_____

_____

_____

_____

_____

_____

_____

_____

_____

A faithful man will be richly blessed, but one eager to get rich will not go unpunished.—PROVERBS 28:20

❧ *November 24*

_____

_____

_____

_____

_____

_____

_____

_____

Now if we are children, then we are heirs—heirs of God and co-heirs with Christ, if indeed we share in his sufferings in order that we may also share in his glory.—ROMANS 8:17

❧ *November 25*

My son, do not despise the Lord's discipline and do not resent his rebuke, because the Lord disciplines those he loves, as a father the son he delights in.—PROVERBS 3:11,12

❧ *November 26*

I am the good shepherd. The good shepherd lays down his life for the sheep.—JOHN 10:11

November 27

_____

_____

_____

_____

_____

_____

_____

_____

_____

The Lord is my rock, my fortress and my deliverer; my God is my rock, in whom I take refuge. He is my shield and the horn of my salvation, my stronghold.—PSALM 18:2

November 28

_____

_____

_____

_____

_____

_____

_____

_____

_____

If you obey my commands, you will remain in my love, just as I have obeyed my Father's commands and remain in his love.—JOHN 15:10

∾ *November 29*

_____

_____

_____

_____

_____

_____

_____

_____

For the Son of Man came to seek and to save what was lost.
—LUKE 19:10

∾ *November 30*

_____

_____

_____

_____

_____

_____

_____

_____

....

December

Tarry at the promise till God meets you there. He always returns by way of His promises.

....

Know that the Lord has set apart the godly for himself; the Lord will hear when I call to him.—PSALM 4:3

∾ *December 1*

_____

_____

_____

_____

_____

_____

_____

_____

_____

_____

For you died, and your life is now hidden with Christ in God. When Christ, who is your life, appears, then you also will appear with him in glory.—COLOSSIANS 3:3,4

∾ *December 2*

_____

_____

_____

_____

_____

_____

_____

_____

_____

_____

Honor the Lord with your wealth, with the firstfruits of all your crops; then your barns will be filled to overflowing, and your vats will brim over with new wine.—PROVERBS 3:9,10

❧ *December 3*

That is why I am suffering as I am. Yet I am not ashamed, because I know whom I have believed, and am convinced that he is able to guard what I have entrusted to him for that day.—2 TIMOTHY 1:12

❧ *December 4*

Those who trust in the Lord are like Mount Zion, which cannot be shaken but endures forever.—PSALM 125:1

❧ *December 5*

"Honor your father and mother"—which is the first commandment with a promise—"that it may go well with you and that you may enjoy long life on the earth."—EPHESIANS 6:2,3

❧ *December 6*

---

f anyone would come after me, he must deny himself and take up his cross and follow me. For whoever wants to save his life will lose it, but whoever loses his life for me will find it.—MATTHEW 16:24,25

December 7

The Lord is far from the wicked but he hears the prayer of the righteous.—PROVERBS 15:29

December 8

Are not all angels ministering spirits sent to serve those who will inherit salvation?—HEBREWS 1:14

∾ *December 9*

_____

_____

_____

_____

_____

_____

_____

_____

_____

Since we have these promises, dear friends, let us purify ourselves from everything that contaminates body and spirit, perfecting holiness out of reverence for God.—2 CORINTHIANS 7:1

∾ *December 10*

_____

_____

_____

_____

_____

_____

_____

_____

_____

_____

With God we will gain the victory, and he will trample down our enemies.—PSALM 60:12

❧ *December 11*

_____

_____

_____

_____

_____

_____

_____

_____

_____

_____

This is love: not that we loved God, but that he loved us and sent his Son as an atoning sacrifice for our sins.—1 JOHN 4:10

❧ *December 12*

_____

_____

_____

_____

_____

_____

_____

_____

_____

_____

And we know that in all things God works for the good of those who love him, who have been called according to his purpose.
—ROMANS 8:28

❧ *December 13*

_____

_____

_____

_____

_____

_____

_____

_____

_____

_____

The Lord sends poverty and wealth; he humbles and he exalts. He raises the poor from the dust and lifts the needy from the ash heap.
—1 SAMUEL 2:7,8

❧ *December 14*

_____

_____

_____

_____

_____

_____

_____

_____

_____

_____

*But if we walk in the light, as he is in the light, we have
fellowship with one another, and the blood of Jesus, his Son,
purifies us from all sin.*—1 JOHN 1:7

❧ *December 15*

Blessed are the pure in heart, for they will see God.—MATTHEW 5:8

❧ *December 16*

You will seek me and find me when you seek me with all your heart.—JEREMIAH 29:13

❧ *December 17*

_____

_____

_____

_____

_____

_____

_____

_____

_____

Once you were not a people, but now you are the people of God; once you had not received mercy, but now you have received mercy.
—1 PETER 2:10

❧ *December 18*

_____

_____

_____

_____

_____

_____

_____

_____

_____

_____

But he was pierced for our transgressions, he was crushed for our iniquities; the punishment that brought us peace was upon him, and by his wounds we are healed.—ISAIAH 53:5

❧ *December 19*

_____

_____

_____

_____

_____

_____

_____

_____

_____

Let us hold unswervingly to the hope we profess, for he who promised is faithful.—HEBREWS 10:23

❧ *December 20*

_____

_____

_____

_____

_____

_____

_____

_____

_____

The Lord is close to the brokenhearted and saves those who are crushed in spirit.—PSALM 34:18

∾ *December 21*

_____

_____

_____

_____

_____

_____

_____

_____

_____

The one who sows to please his sinful nature, from that nature will reap destruction; the one who sows to please the Spirit, from the Spirit will reap eternal life.—GALATIANS 6:8

∾ *December 22*

_____

_____

_____

_____

_____

_____

_____

_____

_____

You did not choose me, but I chose you...to go and bear fruit—
fruit that will last. Then the Father will give you
whatever you ask in my name.—JOHN 15:16

❧ *December 23*

_____

_____

_____

_____

_____

_____

_____

_____

_____

_____

For to us a child is born...and he will be called
Wonderful Counselor, Mighty God, Everlasting Father,
Prince of Peace.—ISAIAH 9:6

❧ *December 24*

_____

_____

_____

_____

_____

_____

_____

_____

_____

He came to that which was his own, but his own did not receive him. Yet to all who received him, to those who believed in his name, he gave the right to become children of God.—JOHN 1:11,12

❧ *December 25*

_____

_____

_____

_____

_____

_____

_____

_____

_____

If any of you lacks wisdom, he should ask God, who gives generously to all without finding fault, and it will be given to him.—JAMES 1:5

❧ *December 26*

_____

_____

_____

_____

_____

_____

_____

_____

_____

My sheep listen to my voice; I know them, and they follow me. I give them eternal life, and they shall never perish; no one can snatch them out of my hand.—JOHN 10:27,28

❧ *December 27*

_____

_____

_____

_____

_____

_____

_____

_____

_____

He will respond to the prayer of the destitute; he will not despise their plea.—PSALM 102:17

❧ *December 28*

_____

_____

_____

_____

_____

_____

_____

_____

_____

_____

We shall not all sleep, but we shall all be changed—in a flash, in the twinkling of an eye, at the last trumpet. For the trumpet will sound, the dead will be raised imperishable, and we will be changed.
—1 CORINTHIANS 15:51,52

❧ *December 29*

_____

_____

_____

_____

_____

_____

_____

_____

You, O Lord, keep my lamp burning; my God turns my darkness into light.—PSALM 18:28

❧ *December 30*

_____

_____

_____

_____

_____

_____

_____

_____

_____

_____

am coming soon. Hold on to what you have, so that no one will take your crown.—REVELATION 3:11

December 31

The Power of the Promises

BLESSINGS OF GOD

For the Lord God is a sun and shield; the Lord bestows favor and honor; no good thing does he withhold from those whose walk is blameless.

PSALM 84:11

But seek first his kingdom and his righteousness, and all these things will be given to you as well.

MATTHEW 6:33

Delight yourself in the Lord and he will give you the desires of your heart.

PSALM 37:4

He who did not spare his own Son, but gave him up for us all—how will he not also, along with him, graciously give us all things.

ROMANS 8:32

Blessed is the man who makes the Lord his trust, who does not look to the proud, to those who turn aside to false gods.

PSALM 40:4

Blessed are the poor in spirit, for theirs is the kingdom of heaven. Blessed are those who mourn, for they will be comforted. Blessed are the meek, for they will inherit the earth. Blessed are those who hunger and thirst for righteousness, for they will be filled. Blessed are the merciful, for they will be show mercy. Blessed are the pure in heart, for they will see God. Blessed are the peacemakers, for they will be called sons of God. Blessed are those who are persec ed because of righteousness, for theirs is the kingdom of heaven.

MATTHEW 5:3-

COMPASSION AND COMFORT

Praise be to the God and Father our Lord Jesus Christ, the Father o compassion and the God of all comfort, so that we can comfort those in any trouble with the comfort we ourselves have receive from God.

2 CORINTHIANS 1:

As a father has compassion on hi children, so the Lord has compas- sion on those who fear him.

PSALM 103:

The Lord is gracious and compassionate, slow to anger an rich in love.

PSALM 145

You will again have compassion us; you will tread our sins underfo and hurl all our iniquities into the depths of the sea.

MICAH 7:

God's Promises for Every Day

f you return to the Lord, then your brothers and your children will be shown compassion by their captors and will come back to this land, for he Lord your God is gracious and compassionate. He will not turn his face from you if you return to him.

2 CHRONICLES 30:9

COURAGE

Wait for the Lord; be strong and take heart and wait for the Lord.

PSALM 27:14

Be strong and take heart, all you who hope in the Lord.

PSALM 31:24

DISCIPLINE

Blessed is the man who God corrects; so do not despise the discipline of the Almighty.

JOB 5:17

Because the Lord disciplines those he loves, and he punishes everyone he accepts as a son. Endure hardship as discipline; God is treating you as sons. For what son is not disciplined by his father? No discipline seems pleasant at the time, but painful. Later on, however, it produces a harvest of righteousness and peace for those who have been trained by it.

HEBREWS 12:6, 7, 11

Blessed is the man you discipline, O Lord, the man you teach from your law.

PSALM 94:12

My son, do not despise the Lord's discipline and do not resent his rebuke, because the lord disciplines those he loves, as a father the son he delights in.

PROVERBS 3:11, 12

ENEMIES

But I tell you: Love your enemies and pray for those who persecute you.

MATTHEW 5:44

I call to the Lord, who is worthy of praise, and I am saved from my enemies:

2 SAMUEL 22:4

Rather, worship the Lord your God; it is he who will deliver you from the hand of all your enemies.

2 KINGS 17:39

If your enemy is hungry, give him food to eat; if he is thirsty, give him water to drink. In doing this, you will heap burning coals on his head, and the Lord will reward you.

PROVERBS 25: 21, 22

ENVY

Let us not become conceited, provoking and envying each other.

GALATIANS 5:26

Do not envy a violent man or choose any of his ways.

PROVERBS 3:31

ETERNAL LIFE

I write these things to you who believe in the name of the Son of God so that you may know that you have eternal life.

1 JOHN 5:13

For God so loved the world that he gave his one and only Son, that whoever believes in him shall not perish but have eternal life.

JOHN 3:16

Whoever believes in the Son has eternal life, but whoever rejects the Son will not see life, for God's wrath remains on him.

JOHN 3:36

But whoever drinks the water I give him will never thirst. Indeed, the water I give him will become in him a spring of water welling up to eternal life.

JOHN 4:14

For the wages of sin is death, but the gift of God is eternal life in Christ Jesus our Lord.

ROMANS 6:23

FAITH

And without faith it is impossible to please God, because anyone who comes to him must believe that he exists and that he rewards those who earnestly seek him.

HEBREWS 11:6

Therefore, since we have been justified through faith, we have peace with God through our Lord Jesus Christ.

ROMANS 5:1

Listen, my dear brothers: Has not God chosen those who are poor in the eyes of the world to be rich in faith and to inherit the kingdom he promised those who love him.

JAMES 2:5

You will seek me and find me when you seek me with all your heart.

JEREMIAH 29:13

FEAR

Have no fear of sudden disaster or of the ruin that overtakes the wicked, for the Lord will be your confidence and will keep your foot from being snared.

PROVERBS 3:25, 26

Even though I walk through the valley of the shadow of death, I will fear no evil, for you are with me; your rod and your staff, they comfort me.

PSALM 23:

Do not be afraid, little flock, for your Father has been pleased to give you the kingdom.

LUKE 12:3

"Don't be afraid," the prophet answered. "Those who are with us are more than those who are with them."

2 KINGS 6:1

The Lord is my light and my salvation—whom shall I fear? The Lord is the stronghold of my life— whom shall I be afraid?

PSALM 27

So we say with confidence, The Lord is my helper; I will not be afraid, What can man do to me?

HEBREWS 13

For I am the Lord, your God, who takes hold of your right hand and says to you, Do not fear, I will help you.

ISAIAH 41:

now, this is what the Lord
~s—he who created you, O
:ob, he who formed you, O
ᴉel: Fear not, for I have
Ɉeemed you; I have summoned
ᴜ by name; you are mine.

ISAIAH 43:1

‘ORGIVENESS

ʋe confess our sins, he is faithful
d just and will forgive us our sins
d purify us from all
·ighteousness.

1 JOHN 1:9

d when you stand praying, if
ᴜ hold anything against anyone,
give him, so that your Father in
ɑven may forgive you your sins.

MARK 11:25

· I will forgive their wickedness
d will remember their sins no
·re.

HEBREWS 8:12

·rite to you, dear children,
cause your sins have been
given on account of his name.

1 JOHN 2:12

ɘ Lord our God is merciful and
giving, even though we have
ɔelled against him.

DANIEL 9:9

the prophets testify about him
t everyone who believes in him
·eives forgiveness of sins through
name.

ACTS 10:43

ny people, who are called by my
 me, will humble themselves and
ɑy and seek my face and turn
m their wicked ways, then will I

hear from heaven and will forgive
their sin and will heal their land.

2 CHRONICLES 7:14

GOOD DEEDS

Let us not become weary in doing
good, for at the proper time we will
reap a harvest if we do not give up.

GALATIANS 6:9

Remember this: Whoever sows
sparingly will also reap sparingly,
and whoever sows generously will
also reap generously.

2 CORINTHIANS 9:6

Give, and it will be given to you. A
good measure, pressed down,
shaken together and running over,
will be poured into your lap. For
with the measure you use, it will be
measured to you.

LUKE 6:38

For we are God's workmanship,
created in Christ Jesus to do good
works, which God prepared in
advance for us to do.

EPHESIANS 2:10

The King will reply, I tell you the
truth, whatever you did for one of
the least of these brothers of mine,
you did for me.

MATTHEW 25:40

And do not forget to do good and
to share with others, for with such
sacrifices God is pleased.

HEBREWS 13:16

Command them to do good, to be
rich in good deeds, and to be
generous and willing to share.

1 TIMOTHY 6:18

The Power of the Promises

GRACE

For it is by grace you have been saved; through faith—and this not from yourselves, it is the gift of God—not by works, so that no one can boast.

EPHESIANS 2:8, 9

And God is able to make all grace abound to you, so that in all things at all times, having all that you need, you will abound in every good work.

2 CORINTHIANS 9:8

For sin shall not be your master, because you are not under law, but under grace.

ROMANS 6:14

What shall we say, then? Shall we go on sinning so that grace may increase? By no means! We died to sin; how can we live in it any longer?

ROMANS 6:1, 2

For the grace of God that brings salvation has appeared to all men. It teaches us to say "No" to ungodliness and worldly passions, and to live self-controlled, upright and godly lives in this present age.

TITUS 2:11, 12

HEAVEN

Blessed are those who are persecuted because of righteousness, for theirs is the kingdom of heaven.

MATTHEW 5:10

Be careful not to do your acts of righteousness before men, to be seen by them. If you do, you will have no reward from your Father in heaven.

MATTHEW 6:1

But our citizenship is in heaven. And we eagerly await a Savior from there, the Lord Jesus Christ.

PHILIPPIANS 3:20

Now we know that if the earthly tent we live in is destroyed, we have a building from God, an eternal house in heaven, not built by human hands.

2 CORINTHIANS 5:

Not everyone who says to me, Lord, Lord, will enter the kingdom of heaven, but only he who does the will of my Father who is in heaven.

MATTHEW 7:2

HOLINESS

Make every effort to live in peace with all men and to be holy, witho holiness no one will see the Lord.

HEBREWS 12:1

Because by one sacrifice he has made perfect forever those who a being made holy.

HEBREWS 10:1

But you are a chosen people, a royal priesthood, a holy nation, a people belonging to God, that yo may declare the praises of him w called you out of darkness into his wonderful light.

1 PETER 2

There is no one holy like the Lord, there is no one besides you; there no Rock like our God.

1 SAMUEL 2

ONESTY

not steal. Do not lie. Do not
ceive one another.

LEVITICUS 19:11

d that in this matter no one
ould wrong his brother or take
vantage of him. The Lord will
nish men for all such sins, as we
ve already told you and warned
u. For God did not call us to be
pure, but to live a holy life.

1 THESSALONIANS 4:6, 7

OLY SPIRIT

I tell you the truth: It is for your
od that I am going away. Unless
o away, the Counselor will not
me to you; but if I go, I will send
n to you.

JOHN 16:7

when he, the Spirit of truth,
mes, he will guide you into all
th. He will not speak on his own;
will speak only what he hears,
d he will tell you what is yet to
me.

JOHN 16:13

d you also were included in
rist when you heard the word of
th, the gospel of your salvation.
ving believed, you were marked
him with a seal, the promised
ly Spirit, who is a deposit
aranteeing our inheritance until
redemption of those who are
d's possession—to the praise of
glory.

EPHESIANS 1:13, 14

Don't you know that you yourselves
are God's temple and that God's
Spirit lives in you?

1 CORINTHIANS 3:16

And if the Spirit of him who raised
Jesus from the dead is living in you,
he who raised Christ from the dead
will also give life to your mortal
bodies through his Spirit, who lives
in you.

ROMANS 8:11

But the fruit of the Spirit is love, joy,
peace, patience, kindness, goodness, faithfulness, gentleness and
self-control. Against such things
there is no law.

GALATIANS 5:22, 23

HOSPITALITY

Offer hospitality to one another
without grumbling. Each one should
use whatever gift he has received to
serve others, faithfully administering
God's grace in its various forms.

1 PETER 4:9, 10

Do not forget to entertain strangers,
for by so doing some people have
entertained angels without knowing
it.

HEBREWS 13:2

JESUS OUR SAVIOR

Therefore, there is now no condemnation for those who are in Christ
Jesus.

ROMANS 8:1

I am the good shepherd. The good
shepherd lays down his life for the
sheep.

JOHN 10:11

The Power of the Promises

....

But thanks be to God! He gives us the victory through our Lord Jesus Christ.

1 CORINTHIANS 15:57

I have come into the world as a light, so that no one who believes in me should stay in darkness.

JOHN 12:46

Jesus answered, I am the way and the truth and the life. No one comes to the Father except through me.

JOHN 14:6

But now in Christ Jesus you who once were far away have been brought near through the blood of Christ.

EPHESIANS 2:13

He came to that which was his own, but his own did not receive him. Yet to all who received him, to those who believed in his name, he gave the right to become children of God.

JOHN 1:11, 12

JOY

Now is your time of grief, but I will see you again and you will rejoice, and no one will take away your joy.

JOHN 16:22

This is the day the Lord has made; let us rejoice and be glad in it.

PSALM 118:24

A cheerful heart is good medicine, but a crushed spirit dries up the bones.

PROVERBS 17:22

For his anger lasts only a moment, but his favor lasts a lifetime; weeping may remain for a night, but rejoicing comes in the morning.

PSALM 30:5

Then make my joy complete by being like-minded, having the same love, being one in spirit and purpose.

PHILIPPIANS 2:2

LIVING

Commit to the Lord whatever you do, and your plans will succeed.

PROVERBS 16:3

Above all else, guard your heart, for it is the well-spring of life.

PROVERBS 4:23

Because he himself suffered when he was tempted, he is able to help those who are being tempted.

HEBREWS 2:18

Then Jesus said to his disciples: Therefore I tell you, do not worry about your life, what you will eat; or about your body, what you will wear. Life is more than food, and the body more than clothes.

LUKE 12:22, 23

Therefore we do not lose heart. Though outwardly we are wasting away, yet inwardly we are being renewed day by day.

2 CORINTHIANS 4:16

The thief comes only to steal and kill and destroy; I have come that they may have life, and have it to the full.

JOHN 10:10

ise be to the Lord, to God our
vior, who daily bears our
dens.

PSALM 68:19

d we know that in all things God
rks for the good of those who
e him, who have been called
cording to his purpose.

ROMANS 8:28

OVE

I tell you: Love your enemies
d pray for those who persecute
u, that you may be sons of your
her in heaven. He causes his sun
ise on the evil and the good,
d sends rain on the righteous
d the unrighteous.

MATTHEW 5:44, 45

ew command I give you: Love
e another. As I have loved you,
you must love one another. By
all men will know that you are
disciples, if you love one
other.

JOHN 13:34, 35

wever, as it is written: No eye
seen, no ear has heard, no
d has conceived what God has
pared for those who love him.

1 CORINTHIANS 2:9

I command you today to love
Lord your God, to walk in his
ys, and to keep his commands,
rees and laws; then you will live
d increase, and the Lord your
d will bless you in the land you
entering to possess.

DEUTERONOMY 30:16

Dear friends, let us love one
another, for love comes from God.
Everyone who loves has been born
of God and knows God. This is
love: not that we loved God, but
that he loved us and sent his Son as
an atoning sacrifice for our sins.

1 JOHN 4:7, 10

LOVE OF GOD

How great is the love the Father
has lavished on us, that we should
be called children of God! And that
is what we are! The reason the
world does not know us is that it
did not know him.

1 JOHN 3:1

Can a mother forget the baby at
her breast and have no compassion
on the child she has borne? Though
she may forget, I will not forget
you! See, I have engraved you on
the palms of my hands; your walls
are ever before me.

ISAIAH 49:15, 16

Because of the Lord's great love we
are not consumed, for his
compassions never fail. They are
new every morning; great is your
faithfulness.

LAMENTATIONS 3:22, 23

For God so loved the world that he
gave his one and only Son, that
whoever believes in him shall not
perish but have eternal life.

JOHN 3:16

Neither height nor depth, nor
anything else in all creation, will be
able to separate us from the love of
God that is in Christ Jesus our Lord.

ROMANS 8:39

The Power of the Promises

NEW LIFE

We are therefore buried with him through baptism into death in order that, just as Christ was raised from the dead through the glory of the Father, we too may live a new life.
ROMANS 6:4

Praise to be the God and Father of our Lord Jesus Christ! In his great mercy he has given us new birth into a living hope through the resurrection of Jesus Christ from the dead, and into an inheritance that can never perish, spoil or fade—kept in heaven for you.
1 PETER 1:3, 4

Therefore, if anyone is in Christ, he is a new creation; the old has gone, the new has come!
2 CORINTHIANS 5:17

For you have been born again, not of perishable seed, but of imperishable, through the living and enduring word of God.
1 PETER 1:23

I have been crucified with Christ and I no longer live, but Christ lives in me. The life I live in the body, I live by faith in the Son of God, who loved me and gave himself for me.
GALATIANS 2:20

OBEDIENCE

but Samuel replied: Does the Lord delight in burnt offerings and sacrifices as much as in obeying the voice of the Lord? To obey is better than sacrifice, and to heed is better than the fat of rams.
1 SAMUEL 15:22

Dear friend, if our hearts do not condemn us, we have confidence before God and receive from him anything we ask, because we obey his commands and do what please him.
1 JOHN 3:21, 2

For whoever does the will of my Father in heaven is my brother and sister and mother.
MATTHEW 12:5

If you obey my commands, you wi remain in my love, just as I have obeyed my Father's commands an remain in his love.
JOHN 15:1

You did not choose me, but I chos you and appointed you to go and bear fruit—fruit that will last. Then the Father will give you whatever you ask in my name.
JOHN 15:

PEACE

Blessed are the peacemakers, for they will be called sons of God.
MATTHEW 5

When a man's ways are pleasing to the Lord, he makes even his enemies live at peace with him.
PROVERBS 1

You will keep in perfect peace hi whose mind is steadfast, because he trusts in you.
ISAIAH 2

I have told you these things, so th in me you may have peace. In th world you will have trouble. But to heart! I have overcome the world
JOHN 16

God's Promises for Every Day

....

ill lie down and sleep in peace,
you alone, O Lord, make me
ell in safety.

PSALM 4:8

ke every effort to live in peace
h all men and to be holy; without
iness no one will see the Lord.

HEBREWS 12:14

ice I leave with you; my peace I
e you. I do not give to you as
world gives. Do not let your
irts be troubled and do not be
aid.

JOHN 14:27

RSEVERANCE

refore, since we are surrounded
such a great cloud of witnesses,
us throw off everything that
ders and the sin that so easily
angles, and let us run with
severance the race marked out
us.

HEBREWS 12:1

only so, but we also rejoice in
sufferings, because we know
suffering produces
severance; perseverance,
iracter; and character, hope.

ROMANS 5:3-5

ause of the increase of
kedness, the love of most will
w cold, but he who stands firm
he end will be saved.

MATTHEW 24:12, 13

refore we do not lose heart.
ugh outwardly we are wasting
ay, yet inwardly we are being
ewed day by day.

2 CORINTHIANS 4:16

POWER OF GOD

I am the Lord, the God of all
mankind. Is anything too hard for
me?

JEREMIAH 32:27

He said: The Lord is my rock, my
fortress and my deliverer.

2 SAMUEL 22:2

Though I walk in the midst of
trouble, you preserve my life; you
stretch out your hand against the
anger of my foes, with your right
hand you save me.

PSALM 138:7

Wealth and honor come from you;
you are the ruler of all things. In
your hands are strength and power
to exalt and give strength to all.
Now, our God, we give you
thanks, and praise your glorious
name.

1 CHRONICLES 29:12, 13

His divine power has given us
everything we need for life and
godliness through our knowledge of
him who called us by his own glory
and goodness.

2 PETER 1:3

PRAYER

For the eyes of the Lord are on the
righteous and his ears are attentive
to their prayer, but the face of the
Lord is against those who do evil.

1 PETER 3:23

This is the confidence we have in
approaching God: that if we ask
anything according to his will, he
hears us.

1 JOHN 5:14

The Power of the Promises

Then you will call, and the Lord will answer; you will cry for help, and he will say: Here am I.

ISAIAH 58:9

Ask and it will be given to you; seek and you will find; knock and the door will be opened to you. For everyone who asks receives; he who seeks finds; and to him who knocks, the door will be opened.

MATTHEW 7:7, 8

Surely the arm of the Lord is not too short to save, nor his ear too dull to hear.

ISAIAH 59:1

Therefore confess your sins to each other and pray for each other so that you may be healed. The prayer of a righteous man is powerful and effective.

JAMES 5:16

PRIDE AND HUMILITY

Therefore, whoever humbles himself like this child is the greatest in the kingdom of heaven.

MATTHEW 18:4

Pride goes before destruction, a haughty spirit before a fall.

PROVERBS 16:18

But he gives us more grace, that is why Scripture says: God opposes the proud but gives grace to the humble.

JAMES 4:6

Humble yourselves, therefore, under God's mighty hand, that he may lift you up in due time.

1 PETER 5:6

PROTECTION OF GOD

My prayer is not that you take them out of the world but that you protec them from the evil one.

JOHN 17:1:

Blessed is he who has regard for the weak: the Lord delivers him in times of trouble. The Lord will protect him and preserve his life; h will bless him in the land and not surrender him to the desire of his foes.

PSALM 41:1,

For in the day of trouble he will keep me safe in his dwelling; he will hide me in the shelter of his tabernacle.

PSALM 27

The Lord will rescue me from ever evil attack and will bring me safel to his heavenly kingdom. To him l glory for ever and ever. Amen.

2 TIMOTHY 4:

The eternal God is your refuge, a underneath are the everlasting arms. He will drive out your enem before you, saying, Destroy him!

DEUTERONOMY 33:

You, dear children, are from Goc and have overcome them, becau the one who is in you is greater than the one who is in the world.

1 JOHN .

REDEMPTION

He himself bore our sins in his bc on the tree, so that we might die sins and live for righteousness; b his wounds you have been heale

1 PETER 2

Lord redeems his servants; no
will be condemned who takes
ge in him.

PSALM 34:22

now, this is what the Lord says—
vho created you, O Jacob, he
formed you, O Israel: Fear not,
have redeemed you.

ISAIAH 43:1

is how we know what love is;
s Christ laid down his life for
And we ought to lay down our
for our brother.

1 JOHN 3:16

he has rescued us from the
inion of darkness and brought
ito the kingdom of the Son he
s, in whom we have
emption, the forgiveness of sin.

COLOSSIANS 1:13, 14

ESURRECTION

believe that Jesus died and
again and so we believe that
will bring with Jesus those who
e fallen asleep in him.

1 THESSALONIANS 4:14

the Lord himself will come down
heaven, with a loud
mand, with the voice of the
angel and with the trumpet call
God, and the dead in Christ will
first. After that, we who are still
e and are left will be caught up
ther with them in the clouds to
t the Lord in the air. And so we
be with the Lord forever.
efore encourage each other
these words.

1 THESSALONIANS 4:16-18

Listen, I tell you a mystery: We will
not all sleep, but we will all be
changed—in a flash, in the
twinkling of an eye, at the last
trumpet. For the trumpet will sound,
the dead will be raised imperishable, and we will be changed.

1 CORINTHIANS 15:51, 52

Do not be amazed at this, for a
time is coming when all who are in
their graves will hear his voice and
come out—those who have done
good will rise to live, and those
who have done evil will rise to be
condemned.

JOHN 5:28, 29

Dear friends, now we are children
of God, and what we will be has
not yet been made known. But we
know that when he appears, we
shall be like him, for we shall see
him as he is.

1 JOHN 3:2

RIGHTEOUSNESS

For the Lord watches over the way
of the righteous, but the way of the
wicked will perish.

PSALM 1:6

Righteousness exalts a nation, but
sin is a disgrace to any people.

PROVERBS 14:34

The Lord gives sight to the blind, the
Lord lifts up those who are bowed
down, the Lord loves the righteous.

PSALM 146:8

God made him who had no sin to
be sin for us, so that in him we
might become the righteousness of
God.

2 CORINTHIANS 5:21

The Power of the Promises

For in the gospel a righteousness from God is revealed, a righteousness that is by faith from first to last, just as it is written: The righteous shall live by faith.

ROMANS 1:17

SALVATION

My soul finds rest in God alone; my salvation comes from him.

PSALM 62:1

That if you confess with your mouth, Jesus is Lord, and believe in your heart that God raised him from the dead, you will be saved.

ROMANS 10:9

I am not ashamed of the gospel, because it is the power of God for the salvation of everyone who believes; first for the Jew, then for the Gentile.

ROMANS 1:16

This is good, and pleases God our Savior, who wants all men to be saved and to come to a knowledge of the truth.

1 TIMOTHY 2:3, 4

Salvation is found in no one else, for there is no other name under heaven given to me by which we must be saved.

ACTS 4:12

STRENGTH

May he strengthen your hearts so that you will be blameless and holy in the presence of our God and Father when our Lord Jesus comes with all his holy ones.

1 THESSALONIANS 3:13

He gives strength to the weary and increases the power of the weak.

ISAIAH 40:2

It is God who arms me with strength and makes my way perfect. You give me your shield o victory; you stoop down to make me great.

2 SAMUEL 22:33, 3

But he said to me, My grace is sufficient for you, for my power is made perfect in weakness. Therefore I will boast all the more gladly about my weaknesses, so that Christ's power may rest on m That is why, for Christ's sake, I delight in weakness, in insults, in hardships, in persecutions, in difficulties. For when I am weak, then I am strong.

2 CORINTHIANS 12:9,

I can do everything through him who gives me strength.

PHILIPPIANS 4

SUFFERING

Consider it pure joy, my brothers whenever you face trials of many kinds, because you know that the testing of your faith develops perseverance. Perseverance mus finish its work so that you may b mature and complete, not lackin anything.

JAMES 1

For our light and momentary troubles are achieving for us an eternal glory that far outweighs them all. So we fix our eyes not what is seen, but on what is

God's Promises for Every Day

een. For what is seen is
porary, but what is unseen is
nal.

2 CORINTHIANS 4:17, 18

only so, but we also rejoice in
sufferings, because we know
suffering produces
severance; perseverance,
racter; and character, hope.
hope does not disappoint us,
ause God has poured out his
into our hearts by the Holy
it, who he has given us.

ROMANS 5:3-5

u are insulted because of the
e of Christ, you are blessed, for
Spirit of glory and of God rests
ou.

1 PETER 4:14

as good for me to be afflicted
at I might learn your decrees.

PSALM 119:71

is why I am suffering as I am.
am not ashamed, because I
w whom I have believed, and
convinced that his is able to
rd what I have entrusted to him
hat day.

2 TIMOTHY 1:12

RUST

in the Lord and do good;
ll in the land and enjoy safe
ure.

PSALM 37:3

e who know your name will
in you, for you, Lord have
r forsaken those who seek you.

PSALM 9:10

Trust in the Lord with all your heart
and lean not on your own
understanding; in all your ways
acknowledge him, and he will
make your paths straight.

PROVERBS 3:5, 6

The Lord is good, a refuge in times
of trouble. He cares for those who
trust in him, but with an
overwhelming flood.

NAHUM 1:7

Those who trust in the Lord are like
Mount Zion, which cannot be
shaken but endures forever.

PSALM 125:1

WEALTH

Listen, my dear brothers: Has not
God chosen those who are poor in
the eyes of the world to be rich in
faith and to inherit the kingdom he
promised those who love him?

JAMES 2:5

But remember the Lord your God,
for it is he who gives you the ability
to produce wealth, and so confirms
his covenant, which he swore to
your forefathers, as it is today.

DEUTERONOMY 8:18

Keep your lives free from the love
of money and be content with what
you have, because God has said,
Never will I leave you; never will I
forsake you.

HEBREWS 13:5

People who want to get rich fall
into temptation and a trap and into
many foolish and harmful desires
that plunge men into ruin and

The Power of the Promises

destruction. For the love of money is a root of all kinds of evil. Some people, eager for money, have wandered from the faith and pierced themselves with many griefs.

1 TIMOTHY 6:9, 10

Sell your possessions and give to the poor. Provide purses for yourselves that will not wear out, a treasure in heaven that will not be exhausted, where no thief comes near and no moth destroys. For where your treasure is, there your heart will be also.

LUKE 12:33, 34

Command those who are rich in the present world not to be arrogant nor to put their hope in wealth, which is so uncertain, but to put their hope in God, who richly provides us with everything for our enjoyment.

1 TIMOTHY 6:17

Honor the Lord with your wealth, with the first fruits of all your crops; then your barns will be filled to overflowing, and your vats will brim over with new wine.

PROVERBS 3:9, 10

WORD OF GOD

The law of the Lord is perfect, reviving the soul. The statutes of th Lord are trustworthy, making wise the simple.

PSALM 1⁹

For the word of God is living and active. Sharper than any double-edged sword, it penetrates even dividing soul and spirit, joints and marrow; it judges the thoughts ar attitudes of the heart.

HEBREWS 4

Jesus answered, It is written: Mar does not live on bread alone, bu on every word that comes from t mouth of God.

MATTHEW

How can a young man keep his way pure? By living according to your word. I seek you with all m heart; do not let me stray from y commands.

PSALM 119:9

Heaven and earth will pass awa but my words will never pass av

MATTHEW 2⁴

All Scripture is God-breathed ar useful for teaching, rebuking, correcting and training in righteousness.

2 TIMOTHY